SPECI̶A̶ ̶ ̶ ̶ ̶ ̶

THE ULVERSCRO̶
(registered UK cha̶
was established in 197̶
research, diagnosis and treatment of eye diseases.
Examples of major projects funded by
the Ulverscroft Foundation are:-

- The Children's Eye Unit at Moorfields Eye Hospital, London
- The Ulverscroft Children's Eye Unit at Great Ormond Street Hospital for Sick Children
- Funding research into eye diseases and treatment at the Department of Ophthalmology, University of Leicester
- The Ulverscroft Vision Research Group, Institute of Child Health
- Twin operating theatres at the Western Ophthalmic Hospital, London
- The Chair of Ophthalmology at the Royal Australian College of Ophthalmologists

You can help further the work of the Foundation by making a donation or leaving a legacy.
Every contribution is gratefully received. If you would like to help support the Foundation or require further information, please contact:

THE ULVERSCROFT FOUNDATION
The Green, Bradgate Road, Anstey
Leicester LE7 7FU, England
Tel: (0116) 236 4325

website: www.foundation.ulverscroft.com

Janine Marsh is a travel writer and Francophile. Formerly a City banker in London, she now lives in France in a renovated barn — along with several dogs and cats, numerous ducks, chickens and geese, and her husband.

Visit her website at:
www.thegoodlifefrance.com

MY GOOD LIFE IN FRANCE

Janine Marsh takes a day trip to France to pick up some cheap wine. A few hours later, she returns to England, having put in an offer on a rickety old barn in the rural Seven Valleys area of Pas-de-Calais. Giving up her job in London, she moves to France with her husband in order to enjoy the good life there — or so she hopes . . . Between getting to grips with the locals and *la vie Française*, and renovating the dilapidated abode, she starts to realise that there's a lot more to her new home than she could ever have imagined.

JANINE MARSH

◆

MY GOOD LIFE
IN FRANCE

In Pursuit of the Rural Dream

Complete and Unabridged

ULVERSCROFT
Leicester

First published in Great Britain in 2017 by
Michael O'Mara Books Limited
London

First Large Print Edition
published 2017
by arrangement with
Michael O'Mara Books Limited
London

ISBN 978–1–4448–3480–2

Published by
F. A. Thorpe (Publishing)
Anstey, Leicestershire

Set by Words & Graphics Ltd.
Anstey, Leicestershire
Printed and bound in Great Britain by
T. J. International Ltd., Padstow, Cornwall

This book is printed on acid-free paper

Contents

Introduction

Over the years, I've met and interviewed many expats living in France, and they seem to fall into three distinct categories.

Group 1 — Retirees
Retired expats go to France for the good life — wine, food, weather, healthcare, quality of life. Some of them are comfortably off, others less so. They are generally a happy bunch who make the most of what's on offer — even on a budget.

Group 2 — Escapees
Those who are running away from something back home, perhaps a failed marriage or business, or they have lost their job. Going to France may be a long-held dream or not. This group also includes those who seek adventure in foreign lands. From what I see, the escape isn't quite as successful for this lot. The right attitude is needed and some of them don't find the life they seek, and may eventually return whence they came. Others fall under the spell of their new destination.

Group 3 — Lifestyle Changees

Members of this group take a decision to move to France often because they have fallen in love with an area, a village they went to on holiday, a house that they knew could be a home like no other, the quality of life — or all of the above.

In this group of expats, my favourites are those who fall in love with a derelict property that most people wouldn't even think of touching. In the heads of these dreamers is their own personal château (even if it's a farmhouse), a vision of loveliness and a home that they feel they will cherish forever.

They buy old houses the French don't want because it costs a fortune to renovate them and make them watertight and warm. They seek dwellings with acres of land, which look wonderfully picturesque and offer a mental picture of liberating freedom and space away from the madding crowd.

They give up their jobs, homes and ties to family and friends to chase the dream of the good life in France and hope a little luck will come their way. They pack their worldly goods into a lorry, van, trailer or car. They squash confused pets and sometimes children in between suitcases and kitchen paraphernalia and head off into a rose-coloured sunset, cheerfully waving goodbye to their past lives, ready and willing to embrace a new life in France.

Not yet at retirement age they must plan to earn an income — often having to swerve from a previous career path and be imaginative in how to use their skills and homes to earn money.

The fact that their home to be has no water, no electricity and no bathroom doesn't daunt them — they plot and plan a way to live with these little challenges while they resolve them. No roof? No problem! They've never done much DIY before but they buy books and scour the internet for advice on how to re-roof, install windows, build walls, plaster a room and lay a floor . . .

At some point, inevitably, they will realize that the wonderful house they fell in love with is a hovel, a money pit, a demanding creature that is never satisfied. The budget they had has long been swallowed up. They must double whatever figure they thought it would cost to renovate it. The bureaucratic night-mare of registering to live and work in France eats into their very soul.

The acres of land that offered so much freedom become a tiresome slog, requiring constant work: cutting grass, pruning trees, mending fences.

Relationships become strained — each

blames the other for the decision to give up what now seems like the best job in the world, civilization and comfort.

But, eventually, with luck and determination, the obstacles are overcome, the tedious paperwork is completed, the house slowly awakens like a phoenix rising from the flames and the course of happiness is regained.

The most successful expats I've met in this group all share similar qualities — they are very determined, bloody minded, hardworking, pragmatic, sanguine, flexible, and eventually learn to accept that sometimes things just don't go the way they planned. They open gîtes and pop-up restaurants, write books, take on building work, teach English, learn a new skill, often in the creative sphere, and they work hard and earn far less than before, but they are happy.

They are also quite possibly a bit mad.

I am one of them, and this is my story of how I learned to be a successful expat in France.

Janine Marsh

1

One cold, wet day

It was on a cold, wet, grey and depressingly dismal day in February more than ten years ago that I took a day trip to France. It was to change my life.

I had taken a day off work from my job in a bank in London to go to Calais, northern France, to buy wine with my dad Frank and my husband Mark. I lived in south-east London, very close to my dad, so getting to France was easy. We had a choice of boat or train just an hour's drive from home; after the first visit to Calais had proved to be so simple, we took to going regularly. We'd shop at one of the wine superstores, have lunch in the friendly town, mooch around the shops, try the local strong cheeses that can strip the fur off your tongue, and buy delicious cakes you just can't get outside of France. Then we'd catch the boat or train back home. In the early years of the new millennium 'booze cruises', as they were called, were popular with Brits wanting to indulge in French liquids of all kinds. It was before the recession, and ferries crossing the Channel were full of people boasting they'd bought a bottle of wine for the cost of an egg.

On that February day it was cold; sleet was falling as we left London and the sky was a horrible grey colour, like someone had coloured it in with a lead pencil. We were bundled up in heavy coats, hats and gloves, the car heating was on full blast and we wondered if we were ever so slightly mad to go on a day trip to France in weather like this.

We went into the Majestic wine store in Calais. I had decided to introduce Dad to decent French wine to see if I could get him to cut down on the hard stuff he'd started drinking more of. Dad annoyed as many people as he could, which was one of his favourite things to do. He would taste a wine and proclaim as loudly as possible that it was not dissimilar to 'gnat's pee' (he never spat it out, though). Eventually, he bought a case of robust Merlot and I don't doubt the patient sales team heaved a sigh of relief when we left.

On that miserable day, instead of having *moules et frites* (mussels and chips — the most popular dish in northern France) for lunch in Calais as we usually did, we decided to venture further inland. We figured that if

6

we drove somewhere within an hour of Calais, we would find a nice, typically French restaurant where we could enjoy a delicious lunch and have plenty of time to return to catch the ferry back to Dover. We salivated over the thought of a cosy brasserie with a friendly waiter and a chef in the kitchen who ought to have a Michelin star but was only really interested in producing great home-cooked authentic dishes for the locals.

Poring over a map book of France, I randomly picked a little town called Hesdin to be our destination. It looked like it was a reasonable size, with plenty of orange blocks on the map indicating there were quite a few buildings, and I was sure one of them must contain somewhere we could get a decent meal. This was France after all, land of haute cuisine.

We arrived in Hesdin just as every restaurant in town closed to would-be lunchers. It was two in the afternoon.

'Bloody hell,' said my dad in disgust. 'You wouldn't want to live in France, would you!'

We wandered forlornly along the main road of the town, coats pulled hard against the biting wind. We couldn't have cared less that the buildings were actually very pretty, that there were quirky little shops, a beautiful old town hall that dates back to the time of

Charles V, ruler of the Holy Roman Empire and of these parts in the sixteenth century. All we saw was that the blinds were pulled down over the boulangerie windows and closed signs were ubiquitous in the restaurants.

It was rapidly obvious to us that for hungry tourists on a winter's day there was absolutely nowhere to eat. Utterly fed up, we headed back to the cobblestoned central square where our car was parked. En route, Mark stopped to look in an estate agent's window; he was working in the mortgage industry at the time so he always looked at house prices wherever we went. Dad and I halted reluctantly. As we stood there, dejectedly staring at tiny pictures of houses in a window that had streams of sleet hitting it and running down the glass, the estate agent opened the door. He peered at us and said in English (how can they tell?), 'Would you like a cup of coffee? You look frozen.'

My dad was in there so quickly I hardly saw his feet move. He made himself comfortable in the warm office and slurped the coffee that the friendly Frenchman offered him with relish. 'Real coffee, proper coffee, French coffee,' he announced. It was like used engine oil: strong, thick and very dark.

Now he had us, the estate agent, a wily salesman, proceeded to try to sell us a house. He had as much chance of that as we had of meeting a unicorn on the ferry on the way home. A unicorn with a saddle that said, 'Hop on, I'll take you back to England the quick way; you won't have to listen to these two men moaning about how cold it is and how much they are not enjoying the day.' I came to with a start. The estate agent was staring intently at me.

''Ow much moanee do you 'ave?'

'None,' I said. 'I have no money at all.'

'If you 'ad moanee to spend on a 'ouse, 'ow much would it be?'

This went on for several minutes while we thawed out and the Frenchman told us that we had in fact travelled to the Seven Valleys, an area of outstanding natural beauty. Historic, he said. Friendly and lots to do.

'Everything's shut,' said my dad, not unreasonably.

The agent chatted away about the merits of life in France, how a holiday home can work wonders for a family, how this place was an undiscovered gem, how the houses were so cheap, so much so that we may be surprised, and really he was sure we had a bit of 'moanee'.

In the end, I said for a joke, 'If I had a

budget, it would be less than one hundred thousand euros.'

He snorted in disgust. Then he leafed frantically through a plastic folder on his desk. Mark and Dad looked at me as if they had suddenly seen the unicorn I had been daydreaming about.

The estate agent handed me three sheets of paper and said, ' 'Ere you are, three 'ouses for less than one hundred thousand euros.'

We were dismissed; clearly poor Brits don't get two cups of coffee. He wanted us gone. It was 2004 and everyone from the UK was supposed to be rich and buying up all the crappy old houses in France at top prices.

Back in the car we sat and debated where to go next. The map didn't show anywhere that looked bigger than Hesdin for many miles.

'We might as well look at these houses, they're really not that far away,' I suggested. We had to do something, after all. My favourite men had faces like thunder.

Mark arched his eyebrows and stared at me, not in a good way. Not in a my-darling-wife-whatever-you-want-is-fine-for-me way.

'Just for fun,' I added. 'Perhaps we'll be able to find a bar that's open in one of the places where these houses are, or maybe we'll pass one on the way. It's either that or head back to Calais.'

'Bar, open.' Magic words to two cold men. We set off with no intention of taking this jaunt seriously but hoping to find a café that was open somewhere in this very rural hinterland.

For the next thirty minutes we drove through several tiny villages and past what seemed like hundreds of soggy fields in which muddy cows looked miserable. We spotted a church spire or two just about visible in the distance, but with absolutely no sign of life and no shops. Eventually, we arrived at the location of the first house on the list.

It was in a village with just one road, which was lined with tall trees; it was just wide enough for two cars to pass. A narrow stream ran along one side of the road and access to houses was via small individual bridges that crossed the stream. They didn't seem strong enough to take the weight of a decent-sized man, let alone a car. The house we were to look at was over one of those links. Since there was clearly no café or bar, I suggested we have a quick look at the house just for the fun of crossing the bridge. There were ominous moans; the air in the car was as sodden with their misery as the rainy air outside.

11

The house was a long, low farmhouse with whitewashed walls, blue framed windows and a red tiled roof. A typical property of the area; we had passed many like it en route. It was clearly empty and had been for some time; the garden was covered in brambles, there was rubbish strewn about and the remains of a fire blackened the path to the front door. If it had been Halloween, I probably would have walked away, as it looked rather scary. There were no shutters over the windows like there were on most houses in the village, so I could peer right into the front room. I could see that every surface was covered in linoleum, the plastic floor covering that used to be popular in the 1960s. In fact, it looked like someone had imagined what psychedelic vomit might look like and then attempted to reproduce it. Orange, brown and yellow swirls and circles battled with each other to take the title of 'most revolting pattern ever'. Whoever designed it was quite possibly deranged.

That also went for whoever had decorated the room. The lino was on the floor, the walls, the back of the door and the ceiling. It couldn't have been more nauseating if it had tried. It occurred to me that it could have been a serial murderer's den: it looked like a 'kill room' in a TV horror series.

Mark had joined me by now — Dad refused to get out of the car — and he too gazed through the filthy windows.

'Well, who knew it could actually look worse inside than out. You want it?' he asked, laughing as we walked back to the car.

We drove about a mile to find the next house. It was in yet another village with no café, no bar, no shops and no sign of life. Shutters with paint peeling off were closed tight against the bitter, wintery day; wispy plumes of smoke rose feebly from a few chimneys, beaten back by the sleet. It was like a ghost town and, by now, even though it was only early afternoon, it was starting to get dark.

'There it is,' I called to Mark as I finally managed to spot the number of the house we were searching for.

He pulled the car over to the side of the road, next to a rather pretty farmhouse, much like the last one but without the rubbish and the brambles and the bridge. I delayed getting out; looking at houses you don't want in the freezing rain isn't half as much fun as you might think.

Somewhere close by a dog started to bark frantically and the front door of the house next door opened. A thin man with no hair emerged; his thick green jumper had a military look to it and he stood strangely still, his unsmiling face pointed in our direction. It wasn't a friendly stare. Then a woman with short hair and two small children joined him. They all stood there watching us, not moving.

'Just keep going,' I hissed at Mark. 'This is like *The Hills Have Eyes*. They've been practising for this,' and we drove on.

We weren't going to bother with the last house, except that the village it was in was on our route back to the ferry.

To reach it we had to drive just a few miles on through yet more deserted countryside and then to the bottom of a steep hill surrounded by forests and miniature mountains. We were right in the heart of the Seven Valleys and once again there was no café, no shops and no people. In fact, in almost an hour of driving, we had not passed a single place to stop and get something to eat or drink. When I look back on it now, I wonder what on earth made me do what I did next.

In this town there were a few houses, mostly farmhouse style, a huge church and a tiny town hall that had a small number of Christmas decorations hanging forlornly from a tree in the car park, which was empty. The last property on our impromptu viewing schedule was called a *longère*, which meant a rural dwelling according to the French

14

dictionary I had with me. It was perched on the edge of a crossroads a little way up a small hill.

We drove up more of a dirt track than a road and stopped outside a broken gate. This place was not remotely attractive: it had a distinct whiff of abandonment. We couldn't see a lot of the house thanks to the ugly concrete wall that enclosed the front garden, and what we could glimpse certainly wasn't enough to tempt any of us out of the car. But I hesitated. It was sufficient to infuriate Dad, who by this time had had more than enough.

'Can we not just get back to Calais and go home? I'm cold, I'm hungry, I'm bored.'

He was right, we were just wasting time. At least back in Calais town or at the port we could get a cup of hot coffee, and plenty of restaurants were open all day, catering to tourists.

Mark turned the key in the ignition, ready to go and, at that very moment, the door of the house opened, a man emerged and waved at us.

'Hold on a minute,' I said. 'I'll just let him know we don't need anything and then we can be off.'

I spoke a bit of French and I was pretty sure I could explain that we weren't loitering with intent to rob the house, in case the man was wondering why we were sitting outside staring in. I got out of the car and walked up to the gate. The road was muddy and water was gushing down it to the drains at the bottom of the hill. My heels stuck in the soft earth that pretended to be a path to the gate. I heard the door of the car open behind me; Dad got out to have a smoke. The man from the house had walked to the gate by now and, smiling, stuck his hand over the top to shake mine. 'Can I help you?' he said, in an English accent. Here in the middle of nowhere, France.

At that precise moment the rain stopped, just like that. A beam from the setting sun broke through the dull heavy clouds; I felt bathed in a ray of glowing sunlight.

At the bottom of the mucky hill, ducks in someone's garden started quacking, the joyous clamour echoing around the valley like laughter.

Somewhere close by I heard a sheep *baa* gently — it was like a welcome.

The rhythmic, melodious and soothing sound of distant church bells pealed.

It sounded like fate.

'Hello,' I said. 'We've been given these house details by an estate agent in Hesdin and we just thought we'd have a drive by and a quick peek.'

'Blimey, we only put it on the market yesterday,' spluttered the man. 'It's not been dressed up or anything. In fact, my daughter who lives here hasn't even cleaned it and I've just popped in to mop up the leaks and make sure the wind hasn't blown the doors off.'

I heard my dad sniggering behind me.

'Want a cup of tea?' asked the man.

'Yes. Please,' I said, not daring to turn to ask my fellow passengers. 'We would love that.' Even now, I don't know what made me accept the invitation; somehow it just felt right, despite the withering looks I got from Mark and Dad.

2

C'est la vie

I am a Londoner, a cockney, which is the term given to someone born within earshot of the bells of the church of St Mary-le-Bow, Cheapside, central London. I like to think my journey to France was fate, that it began the day that I was born. Firstly, St Mary-le-Bow has a French connection: the land that the church was built on was given to a bishop by William the Conqueror in return for support for his expedition to England in 1066. And we all know how that turned out.

Secondly, my name is French. I was supposed to be Ethel, but fate intervened.

My mother had already decided that if I was a girl I would be named after her favourite aunt, who lived three doors down from the house where my parents had lived in Bermondsey, south-east London, in the 1960s, when they were first married. Ultrasound scans weren't that common when I was born; having a baby was like opening a party bag — whatever turned up was a surprise.

The day I was born, the midwife arrived on her bike and decided Mum needed to go to hospital rather than stay at home as planned. My mum was very petite and Sister Cassidy, the midwife who delivered all the babies in that area, was a bit worried about a home birth for such a skinny woman who seemed very stressed about the whole process. My mother was transported to a hospital, within the sounds of those bells at St Mary-le-Bow. My dad saw nothing to be worried or panicked about and decided to spend the day betting on horses.

In those days men didn't like to get involved in the nitty-gritty of marital partnerships and my father couldn't see what responsibility it was of his to help out. So, while my mother was sweating and shrieking in hospital, my father was sweating and shrieking over the 3.45 horse race at Brighton. Both had a great result.

Mum gave birth to me.

Dad won £50 on a French horse called Janine.

Arriving at the hospital with a bunch of flowers and a packet of Turkish Delight for Mum to 'help her get her strength back', he took one look at me and apparently declared I looked like Winston Churchill and the Michelin Man's very fat, ugly love child. He did, however, win my undying gratitude for insisting I be called Janine after his winning horse (a bit of a rarity for him) rather than Ethel. His argument was that I would be a 'lucky filly' — incidentally, the word comes from the French 'fille', meaning girl.

Dad was a bit of a Jekyll and Hyde character, the life and soul of the party one moment, the moaniest old man you could ever meet the next. He would listen to Duke Ellington followed by the Sex Pistols. He drank the finest wines and the cheapest whisky. He was a bridge master and could outplay almost anyone; other bridge players offered him money to be their partner at tournaments. He could do complicated maths in his head, like a human calculator. He was really smart, could be deeply moody and, if you crossed him, he never forgave you.

My mum passed away a few years before that fateful day trip to France. Her death broke my dad's heart and left a gaping hole in my life and that of my siblings. Dad kept going thanks largely to his love of betting: he was a compulsive gambler who could not resist a wager. As a kid I remember him betting me he could get more chocolate in his mouth than me, or he would challenge me to play cards for my pocket money. We would sit at the table for the chocolate contest; Mum would be tutting in disapproval and trying not to smile. Dad would pick up a chocolate, then I would. It was like a scene from a Western, narrowed eyes, breathing through our noses as our mouths filled with sweet, sickly chocolate.

I always lost.

A 'lesson in life' Dad called it. He studied the racing papers every day from the age of nine to the day he died and was addicted to betting on horses and dogs and just about anything else. With Italian ancestry, he was a slim, dapper man, always impeccably dressed and looked a little like Al Pacino.

Utterly desolate at losing my mum, he started drinking a bit more whisky than was good for him. Remonstrating with him didn't work: he was a rebel all his life and never did what he ought to or what you wanted him to. You either had to trick or tempt him to do what you wanted.

Mum argued with him over the choice of Janine as my name, rather than Ethel, but he was adamant and since she was weak with the efforts of bringing me into the world she gave in. Don't get me wrong, there's nothing wrong with the name Ethel, it's just that it wasn't really me.

My earliest memories are of being told my name was French. I was entranced by the notion that this somehow made me a bit different, that I had achieved a coup in the name stakes. Most girls at school were named after their aunties — Brenda and Betty were popular names. For many years I never met anyone else called Janine.

Unfortunately, being called something that was a bit different didn't hold much sway with school kids. 'Janine cleans the latrines' was the best they could come up with, but it was better than what they did to a poor kid with the surname Pritt. Later, when everyone realized that I was growing very slowly and was always going to be short, I was called Mushroom.

Growing up, it was rare for our family to go on holiday; extra money for luxuries was scarce. If we did go away, it was to caravan parks on the English coast. My memories are of rain falling on the plastic roof window, a very bad band trying to play the music of Donny Osmond or Michael Jackson, and a beach on which the sand mingled with silt and looked and felt like you were paddling in . . . well, you can imagine. Times were hard, and we were poor. So how, you might well ask, did I end up living in rural bliss in France?

Well, it took a few years and a lot of hard work, but the real journey started on that cold, wet, dismal day.

3

Un coup de foudre

'Come in, don't worry about the mud on your shoes,' said the man beckoning us into the house.

It felt a bit like entering Narnia, as we had to go through a small wardrobe-like wooden box that had been erected just inside the doorway. It wasn't unlike a coffin from a Hammer horror movie. Cobwebs floated from the ceiling, torn strips of floral wallpaper with a 1950s vibe limped down the walls; it was a DIY porch job of the very worst kind. Did it ring alarm bells? Yes, it did. Each of us could only enter once the person in front had squeezed through the 'porch' (box) and further on through a tiny door into the main hall.

Much to my surprise, Dad was smiling broadly when we all eventually converged on the other side. I caught his eye and saw a look I knew well. Dad found this all highly entertaining. An ex-builder, he was really going to enjoy tearing this place to pieces. Mark just looked bemused. He is a man who likes things to be clean and tidy; an ex-policeman (he's had many jobs) who likes order, he seemed overwhelmed by the clutter and multiple colours of the room we found ourselves in.

The hall had a sticky carpet with a hideous black and orange pattern; it was a sickening configuration that wasn't unlike the vomit-inducing lino we'd seen in the previous house. Our shoes made sucking noises as the carpeted floor was so damp. The walls were a mix of dull grey concrete blocks, the sort that has little holes, perfect for bugs to live in, and off-white chalk blocks and chipboard. A faded lamp in the corner of the dreary and dingy hall revealed that, when we breathed out, it was so cold our breath froze and hung on the air.

There were three doors leading off the hall: one was a hobbit-sized glass door at the top of a step that was almost half a metre high. The other two doors were wooden with frosted amber glass panels that cast a strange orange glow in the room. Next to one of the doors there was a set of stairs. An old-looking dark wood cabinet leaned along one wall and even in the lacklustre light you could see it was riddled with woodworm: every inch of it was covered in oddly sized cups and china items. A small, square, dark wooden table and four chairs were in the centre of the hall, which was also, it seemed, the dining room.

'I'll make a pot of tea,' said the man. 'But do you want to look around first?'

I knew that I ought to say, 'No, thanks, this house looks like it contravenes the Sale of Goods Act by pretending to be somewhere that people can live. I am not sure that I would let a goat dwell here, let alone me.'

But what I actually said, and even I noticed the air of surprise in my voice, was, 'Yes, please, that would be lovely. I'm Janine, this is my dad Frank and my husband Mark.'

Mark looked at me as if he had no idea who I was. Our house in London was neat, tidy, clean, warm and comfortable. We were city folk; mud didn't enter our lives — ever. We once went to Cornwall for a weekend to stay at a farm B&B and we came home early because we didn't like the smell of the country. We woke up on the second morning and I said, 'Can you smell cows?' And Mark said with relief, 'I thought it was me — not smelling like a cow, but, you know.' So we returned to the civilization of city life knowing that living in the country would never be for us.

The man introduced himself as William, and he explained that he checked on the house for his daughter, who was in the navy.

She was engaged to a Frenchman from the area and had bought the house to be near him, but as he was moving south because of his job as an engineer, his daughter was selling up. 'So we'll start upstairs, shall we? You'll have to mind the steps, they're a bit narrow.'

A bit narrow? This staircase was not meant for humans — pixies and elves, maybe. At over 6 feet tall Mark had to go up on all fours like an ape. The steps were high, and as wide as a drawer in a kitchen cabinet. The stairs wove round and up through a trapdoor on to the floor above. I went up first, and at under 5 feet tall even I had to stoop. I watched as Mark emerged — he looked like a giant angry rabbit popping up through a hole.

Dad came up the stairs gingerly, followed by William, and the four of us stood on a sheet of plywood thrown across very warped floor joists. The walls were made of concrete blocks; it looked like a building site, one that had been abandoned many years ago. The upstairs basically formed one room, which ran almost the entire length of this very long narrow house. It was dark; a lone light bulb cast a faint yellow glow over the filth. Cobwebs were everywhere, attaching themselves to our clothes and Mark's head — being the tallest, he was in the firing line.

The loft smelled of animal urine and something else I couldn't identify. The wind howled through a gaping hole in the roof.

There was a large wooden box in the corner by the stairs. It looked a bit like the porch-cupboard downstairs but this one had a sliding door: it was clearly the work of the same builder/bodger.

'This is the *salle de bain*,' said William, gesturing at the box.

The floor bounced ominously under our feet as we made our way over to the so-called bathroom, essentially a wooden crate with a vibrant turquoise-coloured sink that clashed with a lemon-coloured shower unit. A lonely 'Save the Wildlife' sticker clung to the grubby, definitely-seen-better-days (many years ago) shower base. The chipboard walls had nails tacked in to act as pegs to hold the towels. A bare bulb hung down, its wires tangled.

'That's dangerous, that is.'

At last someone had broken the silence. It was hard to know what to say that wouldn't offend but Dad wasn't worried about that.

'That bulb,' he went on. 'If you got water on that . . . BANG,' he shouted, making everyone jump and the floor move up and down wildly. It was like standing on a trampoline and I felt as though the four of us

27

could fall through to the floor below at any time.

'Well,' said William reasonably, 'no one showers much in this house . . . too cold!'

I couldn't look at my dad.

We made our way carefully down the stairs, across the hall and into another tiny concrete room. There was a rusty washing machine and a few pastel pink metal shelf units, the last resting place of several enormous spiders. William kicked the carcass of a long departed bird out of the way and announced, 'This is the utility room.'

Above my head an open pipe jutted into the room, over the end of which was an old wire basket — to stop the rats getting in, explained William, as if it was the most normal thing in the world. The smell of damp was overwhelming. Bad everywhere in the house, in here it reached a peak. The floor oozed with liquid that dripped out of the walls. This surely had to be the worst room in the house.

'The bedroom,' said William as he led us through a doorway that Mark had to stoop under to get through. At this point even William seemed to find it hard to drum up any enthusiasm.

Possibly inspired by a sort of French chalet look, almost the entire room from top to bottom was covered with aged, orange-coloured tongue-and-groove wooden planks.

It was dark, grim, dirty and dank. The word hideous was invented for this house.

There was, though, a flicker of hope. One wall was made from huge chunks of flint stone. It was, among the squalor, quite beautiful.

'Did you do that?' I asked.

'No,' said William. 'Parts of the house are hundreds of years old. This room would have been where people lived, while their animals would have been in the room adjoining.'

Ah, that's what the smell was that I couldn't identify earlier. Damp animal.

The flint stone wall had wooden beams embedded into it and two small windows that looked on to outbuildings in a narrow courtyard. I could see that darkness was falling — as was the rain. I knew we really ought to get a move on and get back to Calais to go home.

We went rapidly through the remaining rooms, each one terrible — not one was habitable, at least not to our standards, and it wasn't possible to call any of them attractive.

'We have to go,' said Mark. 'We need to get back to Calais to catch the ferry.' He had a note of desperation in his voice.

'Yes,' said my dad, 'and I want a fag.'

'Just one more room,' said William. 'The kitchen is right through here and then I can make that pot of tea.'

It was long and very yellow, with a sad old coal oven attempting, not very successfully, to give out some heat. There was a chipped sink, the cheapest of cheap kitchen units, a filthy floor and a door at the other end leading to who knew what. On one wall was the hobbit door that led back into the hall. Opposite that, an enormous picture window that overlooked the garden took up half of the entire wall.

And that is when it happened.

I stood there peering out into the gloom and experienced what the French call *un coup de foudre*, a lightning bolt, love at first sight.

I fell head over heels in love. Completely and utterly bowled over. You're thinking that the garden must have been like Claude Monet's garden in Giverny, aren't you? A picture of lush beauty. Fountains and flora to fall in love with. It wasn't. It was basically two fields with a few trees and a sheep wandering around. It was very green and very big. That was it. Even now I don't know what happened to me that day.

Into my head, entirely uninvited, popped an image of a beautiful vegetable garden and me with a basket full of tomatoes wandering into a kitchen where my beloved would have a glass of red wine awaiting me after my green-fingered efforts.

'We really have to go; seriously, don't worry about the tea, William,' Mark said as he interrupted my reverie.

I turned slowly to look at him. Right in the eyes.

He shuddered and shook his head. He knew that look. He'd seen it before in shops when I wanted to buy something he hated.

'No,' he said. 'No way.'

I just kept looking at him. I was willing him to feel my passion, a sudden, all-encompassing, engulfing, overwhelming ardour for the smelly house and the bleak garden.

Dad, meanwhile, oblivious to my seething desire and the paroxysm of doom that had gripped Mark, had got out his front door keys and was jabbing them into an oak beam that ran up one wall.

'It's rotten that,' he said. 'This house will fall down soon.'

Mark and I continued to stand there looking at each other in silence. It felt as if time was standing still.

'Look at this,' Dad continued. 'Dry rot and wet rot in one room.' He sounded pleased to have made such an interesting and rare discovery.

'This is so shit,' he went on as he pulled a wire out of the wall. 'And I really do love this bit: one little tug and the whole lot will come down on top of us.' He had opened the door at the end of the room to reveal another filthy area, more of a shed, and was pointing to a pole that was in the middle of a doorway without a door. Dad was right: the slim metal bar seemed to be holding up the end of the house.

I knew nothing about the village, the area, the department (the French word for an administrative area, of which there are currently more than ninety in France) or the region the house was in. We had no money to spare. We had not made plans to own a house in France. We hadn't discussed it. Yet, I just knew that somehow, for some reason, this house was meant to be mine.

'Thank you so much for your time,' I said to William as we left. 'I really like the house.' Dad snorted loudly and winked at me with exaggeration as we headed out the front door.

Mark was very quiet all the way home. I said nothing of the fervour that had gripped me. Dad went on and on about how awful the house was.

The next day I emailed the estate agent to find out if there was room for negotiation.

4

Sign here on the dotted line

Very early in the morning on a Wednesday in late May, three months after we had first seen the house, the sun was shining. It was warm and mellow, the sort of day when you wake up and feel like everything in the world is good. Mark and I were off for yet another day trip to France. But this wasn't any old day trip. We were going to sign the final pieces of paperwork that would make us the proud owners of a house in France.

I confess, it was an impulse buy. Not a pair of shoes or a handbag, like most women. It was, in fact, a whole house and an acre of land, and not only that, it came with some extreme building problems that needed sorting out *tout de suite*.

It had been surprisingly easy to buy the property once we had made up our minds to do it (well, once I had made up Mark's mind to do it). I needed to convince Mark that having a second home in France was a good idea. I talked about how a French holiday home would be the perfect getaway, how it might even be somewhere to retire to in the future, many years away. I suggested what we would do to improve things, such as turn the garden from a muddy field into a productive place where we would one day grow vegetables and roses. It didn't take long until Mark started to get excited about the prospect of transforming the unloved house into a stunning home. He agreed to investigate how much the mortgage would be if we were to seriously consider buying a house we knew we couldn't really afford. He worked out that if we got a French interest-only mortgage, with the rates the way they were (extremely low) and the exchange rate the way it was (very favourable to us), the monthly cost of two hundred euros wasn't much more than we paid for our monthly gym membership and dinner with wine in a good restaurant.

The agent selling the house had told me there wasn't much room for negotiation, but a week after we first saw the house, I made an offer of 90,000 euros, 10 per cent below the asking price. The estate agent emailed back to accept the offer within minutes. Later, our French neighbours laughed and said, 'He saw you coming!'

So, we decided to give up our gym memberships. We accepted that we would need to dismiss all dreams of taking an exotic holiday or going out for dinner ever again. We would need to save all of our money to be able to afford to buy the French house, and pay for the maintenance and the cost of going back and forth to visit it. But we figured that if we made many sacrifices and worked our butts off, it was just about doable and, one day, we would reap the benefits.

We were required to agree in writing to pay for the house and then had ten days to change our minds. Which I did on an almost hourly basis. Could we afford it? How would we manage two houses? In the end, though, my heart won and, as the deadline approached, my hand stayed steady and away from the computer to send an email to pull out. The estate agent recommended a *notaire* (the equivalent of a property lawyer) who also worked for the seller — it's normal in France for both parties to share a single point of administration. We paid a deposit and organized a French mortgage as the interest rate was much lower than anything we could get from a bank in the UK.

Mark and I collected Dad so he could come with us and be part of the big day. He puffed frantically on his cigarette on the way down the path as he was banned from smoking in the car. A different car from the one we had taken to France three months ago.

Everything we had earned up to the time we first saw the house went on paying for our home in London, except for one luxury, Mark's car, a Jaguar, something he had wanted since he was a boy. So, when I suggested to him that he sell his beloved XJ6 British Racing Green pride and joy to help raise the money for a 20 per cent deposit on the house in France, he wasn't exactly thrilled, but after some (a lot) of discussion he agreed to let it go and share my car.

It may sound strange but, in all honesty, I didn't really know Mark that well, even though at this stage we had been together for five years. I had met him when, as a single mum with hardly any money to spare, I had bought an old and decrepit car from a friend of a friend for about the cost of a week's food shop for a family of four. The friend of a friend dropped off a very run-down vehicle at my house and left with the money, while I was left with a car that I found I couldn't start and his parting words: 'It probably needs a tune up: it's not been run for a while.'

So, I went through the local free newspaper, the *News Shopper*, looking for a tune-up company and called the number on the first advert I saw and organized for a mechanic to visit on a Saturday afternoon to take a look.

I opened the door to a tall, bearded man with mischievous grey eyes and a crooked smile and it was like a bolt out of the blue; the attraction was instant and profound. The mechanic's name was Mark and mending cars was one of his many skills; he looked at the car I had bought and told me it needed to be scrapped. He was divorced, handsome, funny and passionate. I had been divorced for several years and thought I would never remarry, as I wasn't particularly good at choosing the right man. Mark basically never left. Within weeks he had given up his rented flat and moved into my house in the suburbs of London (one of his other skills is being very persuasive), and we were married not long after.

Mark gave up the car mechanic work and trained as a financial consultant, and we both had jobs that meant that we were spending just a few hours a day and most weekends together, rarely experiencing the intense level of closeness that spending hours on end together brings. Of course, this is the same for many couples, but not really knowing each other that well was to have an extreme impact on us later down the line.

I worried all the way on the drive to Dover,

on the train across to Calais, and on the French roads leading to the little town of Fruges where we were headed for a meeting with the *notaire*. What if it was a mistake? We weren't rich and we'd have to work hard to pay for the house even though it wasn't really expensive — certainly not by UK standards. It seemed like a bargain in many ways: even small houses in London were going for five times that amount and this house had the potential for twenty rooms and it came with an enormous garden.

It was only a year after we bought it that one of my French neighbours told me that the woman who sold it to us had bought it a year before for just 30,000 euros. They had thought she was crazy to pay that much, especially as, two villages along, a house not much smaller was being sold for 5,000 euros. Apparently, the entire village thought we must be very rich to want this rundown dump so much that we would pay, in their opinion, many times what it was worth. For quite a while after that, the farmer who lives at the end of our road slowed down when he saw us and made the 'loads of money' hand signal to us.

Sitting in the waiting room of the *notaire*'s office, I had a niggling feeling of anxiety eating away at me because I'd only seen the house twice. The first time we'd seen it was on that cold day in February; the second time was in March when Dad and I had gone out to take some measurements. My dad had assured me then, with utmost certainty, that it was a money pit and I would be paying out for the rest of my life.

It was done now, though.

While we were in the *notaire*'s office signing away all thought of any luxury for years to come, I had deposited my dad at the Café Aux Trois Pigeons, which perched at the edge of the main square in the town.

We were with the *notaire* for two hours, smiling, initialling what felt like hundreds of bits of paper, nodding and doing as we were told while not really understanding very much at all. The *notaire* checked the money was where it should be and read things out to us in speedy, incomprehensible French. His assistant came in and photocopied reams of paper, and everything had to have signatures in triplicate.

In the back of my mind was the thought of Dad in the bar. By now I was sure he would have moved from drinking coffee to beer and chatting to everyone. He hardly spoke a word of French but he thought that by saying words really loudly, everyone in France would somehow understand him better. 'A BEER,

SEE VOO PLAY' yelled at anyone in any bar in France seemed to my dad to be perfect French. Actually it's close enough to make sense to most French people, but 'DO YOU HAVE NUTS?' not so much. He once shouted 'DO YOU HAVE A PINT OF THEAKSTON'S OLD PECULIER?' in a bar in the hilltop town of Montreuil-sur-Mer, which caused the entire place to come to a standstill.

Eventually, the *notaire* and his assistant stood up, smiled, advised us we were done and shook hands with us. It was midday and, as I came to know later, everything miraculously gets finished in time for lunch, however long the paperwork or however big the problem.

'*Félicitations*, Madame Marsh,' said the *notaire*. '*Bienvenue en France.*'

We hurried to the bar, collected Dad, who thankfully had not caused any problems, and made straight for our new home. I had packed a bottle of champagne and a picnic and was looking forward to celebrating. Now that everything was signed there wasn't much point in worrying and the excitement was building up. Our house is twenty minutes from Fruges, and the drive takes you through beautiful countryside of small woods and fields of cows and wheat, past tiny villages with just a few ancient houses peppered here and there. There are often chickens in the road that scatter when they hear a car approaching, and dogs that run to gates when they hear the chickens clucking.

We drove into our tiny village, past the town hall, up the dirt track hill and stopped outside the broken gate. My heart was thumping as we walked up the path and put the key in the door, entered the dark, damp, smelly hall, climbed up the enormous step clearly made for a giant, into the kitchen and . . . it was like when a record screeches then stops dead.

We hadn't been out to the house for two months. It was now the end of May and it looked as though the seller had simply abandoned it on hearing that the mad English couple were buying her run-down, rickety old house in the middle of nowhere. There were some things missing and other things had appeared that we had never anticipated.

What there wasn't:

Water
Electricity
Light bulbs
Handles on kitchen cupboards
Mobile phone signal

So, we couldn't call the estate agent to ask why there was no water and no electricity after he had promised that it would be organized. For a 10,000 euro fee (in France the buyer pays it, not the seller) we'd expected him at least to sort that out for us.

Of course, this prompted my ever helpful father to immediately, absolutely have to have a cup of tea right now.

What there was:

> Rodent droppings on the kitchen work surfaces
> Waist high grass. We wouldn't be having a picnic in the garden, then
> A caravan. Now, I wouldn't mind if it was a half decent one but this was an old wreck with broken windows, missing its door and it had been left in the middle of the garden
> A sheep. A very large, dirty, smelly one. It was eating the grass outside the kitchen window

'Okay,' I said, taking a deep breath. 'We knew it wasn't going to be perfect. We know there's work to do, but just look at the space out there in the garden. That beautiful willow tree will be perfect to sit under one day. That walnut tree is heavy with luscious fruit. The apple, plum and pear trees are full of deliciousness to come.'

Mark and Dad looked at me. I gulped and carried on: 'This house has so much potential. The lovely beams, the amazing flint stone wall in the bedroom . . . '

Dad cleared his throat and turned to fix his eyes on me.

'This house,' he said, 'is not just a paint-it-and-enjoy-it second home. This house that you've bought in France is a lifetime of renovation and maintenance. This house is not just for Christmas, it's for life.'

He laughed so much he coughed and then reminded me he couldn't even have a cup of tea for his throat, which was dry from laughing.

Not for the first time, I wondered if I had completely lost my mind.

The euphoria of owning a house in France melted away and I came back down to earth with a thump rather than a bump, and spent the afternoon running up the hill trying to get a signal to contact the estate agent to get him to sort out the missing water and electricity.

We celebrated with a picnic in the yellow kitchen and toasted our new home with a bottle of water, as it no longer felt like a champagne moment, and then drove back to

London as Mark and I had to work the next day.

It was really only when I went to bed that night back home, and lay awake thinking about the day, that it dawned on me just what an enormous task lay ahead to make that old house even habitable for weekend stays. The argument raged in my mind: I'd bought a massive, unloved barn that had dirt floors, broken windows, doors that didn't lock, holes in the roof and suffered from a really bad damp problem. No, I'd bought a beautiful French barn with huge potential, part of which dated back hundreds of years and had the most gorgeous beamed ceilings in one or two of the rooms . . . It had an acre of land that was out of control . . . No, it had an enormous garden that would look like a country estate one day . . . It came with a sheep . . .

Hang on a minute, it came with a sheep? In all the rushing around trying to sort out utilities, blocking up broken windows, securing doors that could blow open in a gust of wind and be carried away over the hills, I'd forgotten all about the sheep in the garden. Had the previous owner left it behind? Had it escaped from a farm? Had someone dumped it there?

Unlike most people who count sheep to go

to sleep, it was just a single one that instead kept me awake.

On our next trip we found out that the sheep belonged to an old man in the village. The previous owner of our house had allowed the sheep to be kept in the garden as it kept the grass down. Of course, like everyone else in the village and apparently for villages miles around, the old man knew the house had been sold to a crazy English couple for an outrageous sum of money. One man who came to the door and introduced himself as Olivier, a local, explained to us that the old man wanted to leave the sheep there as he had a much smaller garden. Since the previous English owner had no objection, Olivier told us that the old man hoped we wouldn't either. I immediately agreed for three reasons. It would keep the grass down, it would make the villagers happy to know we were willing to be part of the community, and I liked the sheep.

For two years the woolly creature lived in our garden, eating everything in sight, climbing trees — well, attempting to at any rate; it was a bit confused, I think — and leaving poo everywhere. We called it Trumper on account of the awful smell it gave off.

The old man who owned it never said a word to us and completely ignored me when

I tried to speak to him; not even a smile.

One weekend we arrived at the house and the sheep was gone. The old man was very sick and had taken 'the filthy beast', as the neighbours called it, back into his own garden. He could no longer gather the energy to go and get water for it or check up on his animal, which, in fact, he was very fond of. We too had grown quite attached to Trumper by now, and when it left we would feed it carrots through the gate at the old man's house. Before he died, the old man stipulated that one of his last wishes was that whoever bought his house must allow the sheep to live in the garden. The unsuspecting family who moved in after his death went along with this strange requirement, feeling sure that it would only be for a short while. After all, the sheep was at least twenty years old if the villagers were to be believed — or about 140 in human years. It lived for a further four years and was known as the oldest sheep in the country, according to Olivier.

Sometimes when you buy a French house, you get more than bricks and mortar.

5

Summer in the Seven Valleys

For the rest of that first summer of 2004 when Mark and I became home owners in France, we spent as many weekends as we could in the Seven Valleys. Sometimes we went in the car, taking my dad with us, and sometimes we went alone on our motorbike. We found quick ways to get from London to Dover and from Calais to our village and discovered that we could pretty much do the entire journey in just three hours.

At least, most of the time. One Friday night in late July, after a day in the office, we left London by bike under ominous dark skies. When we emerged from the tunnel in Calais we were met with torrential rain, thunder and lightning. Pulling on our gloves and doing our coat collars up, we headed into the wetness and aimed for our village. Somehow we missed a turning and ended up off course and in the forest outside the port town of Boulogne-sur-Mer, just twenty minutes from Calais. It's a huge area of hills and forests, quite beautiful during the day and popular with walkers, but at night, when you're lost in a storm, it resembles a place you might see in a scary movie.

By now it was almost midnight, pitch black apart from when the sky was scratched by vivid wild lightning streaks. The bike intercom system we used to talk to each other had died — it had drowned, I think. I had visions of us being eaten by wild pigs and our bodies being discovered by gendarmes a few weeks later.

This is not me being overdramatic; there are plenty of wild boars in parts of France and I've often seen them run across fields. Great big hairy creatures, they're quite shy but, if scared, can be aggressive.

Thankfully, on that dark night in the woods, it wasn't our time to go. Mark managed to find his way back on to a main road and we arrived home, bedraggled and utterly fed up. My gloves were so sodden they disintegrated. My boots were full of water. We simply dried off and fell into bed to sleep off the stress of the journey.

In the morning, the sun returned, and streamed in through the windows, which I threw open to breathe in the scent that comes after a downpour in the country. Grass and blooming flowers are a heady combination in this sweet pure air. The perfume chased away the memories of the horrible journey of the night before. I could hear Thierry the farmer firing up his tractor at the top of the hill and a couple of minutes later he drove past dragging a trailer load of manure — the other scent of the country.

The house started to reveal itself to us as we spent time there and I wish I could say that there were hidden treasures — secret marble fireplaces and fabulous delights. Sadly, that wasn't to be. Upstairs was completely uninhabitable, dirty, dark and open to the elements, with gaping holes in the walls as well as the roof. We simply closed the trapdoor at the top of the stairs and left it alone. It was a bit like a submarine hatch and at least it kept out some of the draughts, bugs and animals that lived there. Downstairs was just about endurable. We camped in the room with the flint stone wall and Dad camped in the front room. Cooking was done on a barbecue in the garden, whatever the weather. At one end of the house was the room with no door and a pole holding things up. At the other end, matching it in hideous style, was a room that had only two walls, which were covered with a plastic roof. We used it as an outdoor dining area, dragging our little barbecue under cover when it rained.

Our main job that summer was to clear out

the rubbish in the house and keep the garden under control. We went through each room, getting rid of sticky carpets, old beds, fridges, piles of newspapers from the 1970s, broken tiles and assorted trash. As we went along I painted all the walls white, including the concrete blocks, in an attempt to make it look a bit better. In reality it looked more like a prison than a holiday home.

Spending short stints in your second home abroad once in a while doesn't really give you a full sense of what real life is like in a new country. We met the neighbours occasionally and they seemed pleasant and friendly, if a bit aloof. Most of our encounters at this stage consisted of nodding to each other.

Friends and family came to visit and were shocked by the state of the house. This was no Provençal dream barn, after all; staying with us meant roughing it. With no shops or bars in the village it can feel really quite isolated. Some people, however, fell under the spell of the slower pace of life, the fabulous chocolate shops and boulangeries in the nearby town of Montreuil-sur-Mer, which smelled of freshly baked croissants and baguettes, and the vibrant street market in Hesdin, which we discovered was nothing like the dull place we had thought it was that grim February day when we ended up there. It was hard not to love the cafés in Hucqueliers, the sheer gastronomic delight of French life and the history and heritage of this part of northern France. Everyone was captivated by the fact that we could buy fresh goats' cheese straight from the farm down the road, and the weekend flea markets won many fans among our visitors. Dad liked to try the different foods: locally made hams, honeys and jams, though he baulked at snails and turned down crispy fried frogs' legs in the Chinese restaurant in Saint-Omer.

Some people were amazed by the amount of land we had, and Mark's sister Loraine and brother-in-law Martin adored it; they dreamed of one day buying a house close by. Like us, they had lived their whole lives in London and relished the space, the sheer vibrant greenness of the lush countryside of this part of northern France and the fact that you could drive for miles without passing another car.

Whoever came out invariably got roped in to help with renovating and gardening. At the end of the summer, the house started to feel less like a shed and more like a shed with a little bit of soul (if you narrowed your eyes and were in an optimistic mood).

Dad's prediction that having a second home was a never-ending chore started to come true. There was always so much to do: on every visit the grass needed to be cut, weeds had started to take over and the damp in the house had got worse, but we made time to explore.

Not too far away, there's another very small village, quite pretty with a handful of houses and two commercial buildings. One is a traditional butcher's shop and sells fresh meat from local farms and charcuterie prepared by the shop owner. The other is opposite, a run-down building with a big car park; it's a cross between a house and a hut, grubby and worn out. It has a hand-painted sign, strung haphazardly across a window, stating that it is a 'Club Privé'. Mark and I assumed that this was a sort of pub or club. We'd passed this place several times and thought it might be fun to go there, perhaps with Dad.

One day, we were working in the front garden and some elderly neighbours wandered past and invited us to come and have a beer when we finished. They introduced themselves as Stefan and Babette, originally from Lille. They told us that they lived in the road by the chapel, which we would know by the gnomes in the front garden. So we headed to their house on a beautiful summer evening, 6 p.m. being the time for apéritifs in these parts. They were friendly and we were soon laughing away as if we'd known each other a lot longer. I mentioned to them that we were thinking of popping down to 'Le Club Privé' when we next came out and did they want to come with us?

An ominous silence fell in the room. Babette looked at the floor, Stefan looked at me open-mouthed. Nothing was said for what felt like several long seconds.

'Look', I said, 'it was just a thought, maybe another time.'

Again silence.

'Or,' I offered, wondering what on earth I must have said to cause such a weird reaction, 'you could come to us instead. We'll bring some English beer.'

Stefan cleared his throat and said, 'We're a little old for that sort of thing these days.'

'What — beer?' I said incredulously, as he was clearly enjoying the glass that Babette had refilled several times.

'No,' he said. '*Libertins*.'

After it became clear that I had no idea what he was talking about, we had a fun conversation that involved the use of a French — English dictionary as I looked up some new words and discovered that *libertin* means someone who is without 'moral or sexual restraints' and the Club Privé was in fact a swingers' club. Apparently, people come from further away than Paris to party there.

Who'd have thought it, in middle-of-nowhere France? I didn't know whether to be more surprised that it was there at all or that Stefan informed me that he's a bit old for it 'these days'.

One weekend, the surrounding towns were plastered with glossy posters advertising a night of excitement in Aix-en-Issart. This pretty village with a pine furniture shop, a church and a clutch of houses was to host a riveting night of entertainment, fabulous food and 'illuminations', which we translated in our heads as 'thrilling, electrifying light show'. Since we hadn't really seen much evidence of nightlife — the local café-bars in Hucqueliers, as lovely as they are, generally close by 9 p.m. and there didn't seem to be much else close by — we couldn't resist it. Thanks to the expensively printed posters, we were excited to find out more about what we thought must be a truly spectacular event. Lyon and its famous Festival of Lights came to mind. We drove the few miles from our house, along a winding country lane, past a wood mill with its wheel turning gently and farmhouses with shutters closed (as usual there was hardly any evidence of life in the countryside) en route to the town.

Yet on reaching Aix-en-Issart we had to

drive right through and out the other side to park because there were so many cars. On the walk in, the main street was absolutely packed with people. We took this as an indication that we'd stumbled on to a really sensational event. Dusk was falling. Just perfect to be able to see the illuminations, we thought. We followed the crowds along the narrow road to the main square, walking alongside a bubbling stream, its neat grassy banks lined with trees through which a few Christmas tree-style lights were hung. It was very pretty, but hardly the grand illuminations we expected. As we approached the square, I almost fell into the water when a man wearing long boots appeared in the stream as if from nowhere. We stopped to watch him fiddle with something along the top of the water line, cursing under his breath and then sighing with happiness as . . . more fairy lights came on along the side of the stream.

'I think these are the illuminations,' said Mark.

He was right. In those days we were still green townies, used to the bright lights of London and unaware of the less obvious treasures of rural northern France. I confess we were disappointed to start with. In a grand marquee we lined up with red-faced French men buying beer and cider to cool down on the hot summer night. We were warmly welcomed and sat on the plastic chairs in the square, watching as people arrived. We had no idea what to expect but clearly some sort of entertainment was on offer. A makeshift stage had been created on the trailer of a lorry parked on the edge of the square, and spotlights were trained on the 'platform' where drums and musical instruments were set up. More and more people arrived and the chairs rapidly filled.

A group of teenagers marched around playing drums and bongos, dancing and laughing. The atmosphere was one of excitement; an air of anticipation began to build, and there was a sudden intake of breath when an announcement was made by a man walking round with a loud speaker that the highlight of the evening, the moment we had all been waiting for, was here. The lights dimmed, a crescendo of drums echoed round the square, and then the lights went back on. Band members and a singer had stumbled their way on to the stage in the dark and were blinking as the spotlights temporarily blinded them.

The music struck up, French rock style, and the singer began to belt out a number. The audience tapped their feet, nodded their heads, clapped and swayed; a few got up and danced. This region, we were to discover, loves to dance. There are tea dances in many towns and whenever someone starts to play music or a musical instrument — be it in a café or in the street — you can almost guarantee a couple will jump to their feet and foxtrot or cha-cha with abandon.

Ten minutes in and the singer stopped. The band stopped too, abruptly, and we all heard a mobile phone ringing. The singer glared at a man in the audience who was fumbling with his phone, trying to turn it off. The singer resumed.

'Did that really happen?' asked Mark, looking at me in astonishment.

Yes, it did, and the singer halted his act three more times when he felt that his adoring fans were not being adoring enough by giving him their full attention.

By this time we were not just bemused, we were highly amused, as were the rest of the audience, most of whom were by now tucking into moules served from vast saucepans and frites from a mobile wagon. We thought it couldn't get much better when, at the end, as the star was getting ready to perform his last number to wild acclaim, those pesky teenagers started playing the drums again: this time the singer stormed offstage, never to return.

It was, everyone said afterwards around the bar, by the light of the glittering stars and a bright moon, a rather memorable and most enjoyable night.

6

It's as cold as ice

In the winter things were quite different.

From October onwards it started to get cold. At night the clear sky twinkled with thousands of stars and in the mornings heavy frosts made the grass sparkle. Although it was generally not a bad winter, it was our first experience of the season in France and it was nothing like being in London.

The first neighbour we really got to know well was Jean-Claude. We would see him every time we were in France as he drove from his home at the bottom of our hill to his mother-in-law Claudette's farmhouse towards the top of our hill. Now in his fifties, he had been a farmer until a heart attack forced him to take early retirement. He has a ruddy face creased with laughter lines, is short and stocky with a mop of hair combed to the side and thick glasses, and is always dressed in hunting green. Whenever he saw us he would shake hands and comment on the weather. Only later when we became friends with more people in the village did we discover that he is known as 'Monsieur Partout' (Mr Everywhere) because he wanders round the village most of the day, stopping off to say hello to friends and neighbours over a beer or glass of red wine (depending on whether it is eight in the morning or six in the evening).

One wintry November morning, he passed by as we returned from the supermarket in nearby Hucqueliers (which incidentally was where much of the TV series *French Fields* was filmed) and as usual stopped for a chat.

'I think it might snow soon,' I said.

'It never snows in this village, not in decades,' he declared firmly before marching off up the road.

We trundled into the house. Despite having had the wood fire going since the night before, it was still very cold.

We had, at that point, no idea what we were in for.

Our weekend visits had become more infrequent as the winter weather set in, and it snowed despite Jean-Claude's declaration that it wouldn't happen, but we were determined to spend Christmas in France. Dad refused to come. 'Not likely,' he said. 'Too bloody cold. I'm off to your brother's house, nice and warm there.'

On Christmas Eve, I finished work at

lunchtime and caught a train home from London Bridge. We loaded the car with our cases and food and set off for France.

By the time we arrived in the late afternoon it was already pitch black. All the houses in the village had their shutters closed against the chilly night and it looked like the whole place had been abandoned. Fans of *The Walking Dead* might have wondered if the worst had come to pass. Our route from Calais had taken us on the A16 autoroute and then through the countryside, passing a dozen little villages. We were surprised that there were so few Christmas decorations — some sad stars strung across the road here and there, a couple of lamp posts with holly tied to them — otherwise you wouldn't know it was a celebratory time of the year.

In our village, the only sign it was Christmas at all was at the town hall, where a line of coloured lights glowed in a lone tree, swinging wildly in a wind that was starting to howl.

We pulled into our front garden filled with Christmas joy. We unpacked bags of luscious food and bottles of wine and champagne bought at the supermarket at Boulogne-sur-Mer, which is on the way to our house, and put the key in the door. Our festive bubble burst when we opened it and were taken aback to find it was actually colder and damper inside the house than outside. No matter, we thought. We had managed to buy some wood for our enormous fire from a man who stopped at the house with a lorry load. Getting someone to deliver, we discovered, is not always easy, as nearly everyone where we lived had tractors or trailers and collected it themselves, and those wood suppliers who said they would deliver never arrived nine times out of ten. We'd bought 3 tonnes of logs; they were stacked up to the roof in the old pigsty in the garden, enough, we thought, to last us at least a year or two.

Mark lit the fire and I put the kettle on, which caused the lights in the house to dim as usual. We were to discover that, unlike in the UK where you can plug appliances in and they work, in France you pay for a set supply of electricity. We were on the lowest amount, 3 kW, which meant that when we turned the kettle on at the same time as the water heater and lights, it used almost all of the supply for the house and caused the lights to dim. If you turned the hair dryer on as well, everything tripped out. It took us many torch-lit visits to the fuse box to switch it all back on again before we moaned about it to Jean-Claude and he told us that we just had to call the electricity company to increase our tariff.

Four hours later and the house felt a little warmer but not exactly cosy. We had no TV signal but we could play DVDs and were huddled under blankets as close to the fire as we could get without actually burning, watching a film, trying to ignore the fact that it was a bit like sitting in an igloo. An early night loomed and, I have to tell you, it was not romantic: the bed felt damp, the room was frozen — in fact, the heat seemed to stop about 20 centimetres out from the wood fire.

We spent Christmas morning driving up the hill trying to get a mobile phone signal to ring friends and family to wish them well and then returned to the house to cook dinner. As we still had no oven, it was going to be a barbecue with champagne.

We sat in the garden with a patio heater on and laughed at how different this was to our usual Christmas Day in London. We played shuttlecocks and shot at a broom with elastic band guns and talked and talked. There were no distractions other than the cold, and nothing to demand our attention. We decided, though, that it might be best to restrict visits to the warmer months.

That night we went for a walk around the village. There are no street lamps in the little roads and there were no Christmas lights on or signs that it even was Christmas — even the string of lights in the tree by the town hall were switched off. The wind had died down and the clear sky was full of twinkling stars; the more we looked the more we could see, millions and millions of tiny diamonds in the sky. We wandered with a torch, scaring wild pheasants and grouse from under the hedges when the light shone their way. The fields were covered with a delicate dusting of frost that shone softly. Owls hooted, calling to each other across the red tiled rooftops of the village houses, and a few dogs barked as we passed the gardens they protected. Other than that it was truly a silent night. The air was scented with the sweet smell of wood-burning fires of our neighbours. We held hands and walked until our noses felt frozen.

We passed a house where a man had popped outside to put empty bottles into a crate by the front door, ready to go to the village bottle bank in the morning. '*Joyeux Noel*,' he called out, and we wished him a Merry Christmas in return.

Back inside, we were both agreed: though it was neither fun nor pleasant to be damp and cold, as it was in winter in this old building, we would always try to enjoy Christmas Day there. It was a hint at the little corner of paradise we had found for ourselves.

7

Getting to know you, getting to know all about you

For the next four years we spent several weekends a year at our French house, but nowhere near as much as we had that first summer. We fell in love with life in France: the tranquillity and space in contrast to London was alluring. It got harder and harder to go home each time. Sometimes quite literally. It rains a lot in this part of France and occasionally our car got stuck in the mud in the garden. One Sunday night we prepared to return to London and found the car just wouldn't move.

'I'll push, you drive,' said Mark, only to be covered in sludge as the wheels spun furiously, digging deeper into the mud as ferocious rain lashed down and the air boomed in a full-on thunderstorm.

We thought about asking one of the farmers to come and pull us out with a tractor, but it was dark and Sundays with the family in France are sacrosanct and we didn't want to interrupt anyone.

'What a stupid idea,' said Mark when I suggested we pour a bag of cement powder around the wheels of the car and let it harden overnight. But after an hour of trying to come up with something better, that's what we did. In the morning, much to my relief my 'stupid idea' worked and we managed to get back to London in time for work.

The whole point of buying the house had been to enjoy our place in the sun, but what actually happened was that we spent much of the time restraining the rampant growth of grass and hedges. Dad usually came with us to 'help', but only in the summer. Generally speaking, his assistance consisted of telling us what we had done wrong after we'd done it. When we had to cut down a willow tree because the roots were starting to lift up the walls of the house as it had been planted only feet away, Dad was on hand to advise. The tree was huge — my neighbour recalled it being planted fifty years before — and I hated to see it go, but it had to be done. It was a hot day. Mark fired up the chainsaw and climbed a ladder that was propped against the vast trunk. He cut branches while Dad kept a foot on the ladder to steady it and I dragged the branches over to the bonfire area. Mark built a sawhorse to lay the biggest branches on to make them easier to cut; 'time wasting', Dad called it, until he saw Mark's angry, hot, red face and decided to take an afternoon nap.

It wasn't all work, though. We did find some time to start discovering the local area, which, since we had bought the house in the first place knowing nothing at all about it, could have turned out disastrously. It was, in fact, amazingly special. The Seven Valleys turned out to be rural France at its best: sleepy, peaceful villages, uncrowded country lanes, friendly bars and cafés — Dad said that it reminded him of England half a century ago.

The nearest big town is medieval Montreuil-sur-Mer, a walled hilltop time warp of a place, and it became a favourite destination. People come from villages far and wide to shop and meet in cafés and buy fresh vegetables and produce from the market stallholders on a Saturday morning. With its ancient cobbled streets, narrow passageways and stunning old buildings dating back several centuries, it looks like something out of a picture perfect history book and, in some ways, it is exactly that. The great French writer Victor Hugo spent an afternoon there in 1837 canoodling with his mistress in room 12b at the Hôtel de France, which was built in the sixteenth century. Years later his memories of the town, the people he met and the things he saw served as inspiration for his famous novel *Les Misérables*, published in 1862. While there he witnessed a horse-drawn coach crash in the steep street called Cavée Saint-Firmin, which became an important scene in the book; and he made Montreuil the birthplace of one of the lead characters, Fantine, apparently after he saw a sobbing woman emerge from the town's church.

Every summer the people of Montreuil-sur-Mer pay tribute to the great writer and put on a musical version of *Les Misérables* on the ramparts, complete with galloping horses and booming cannons. Around six hundred people take part, making costumes, acting, dancing, singing; it is a joyful and exuberant event. It usually starts at 10 p.m. when the summer sun has sunk below the citadel and everyone has eaten in one of the local cafés and restaurants without rushing (that would be so not French). If you happen to be in the town on a night when a performance takes place, you are likely to see soldiers in nineteenth-century uniform, nuns and milk maids quaffing wine and smoking in the square, or chatting with Victor Hugo who happens to work for the tourist board but bears an uncanny likeness to the town's hero.

It's a lovely place to visit, with a market

that's quintessentially French. Little old ladies sit at foldaway tables with a few vegetables from the garden competing with stalls brimming with lush and exotic fruit; long plaits of locally grown and smoked garlic, pungent cheeses and salty charcuterie. There's a lady who sells underwear that you would expect to see in an Ann Summers sex shop alongside voluminous thick cotton nightdresses that a family of four could live in, as well as artisanal bread and cakes that make you drool.

You can walk round the ramparts just as Hugo did, although many visitors are astounded to discover that there are no railings — with a thirty-metre drop to the bottom of the town. At dusk, watching the sun set through the arrow holes built into the massive stones walls is a must before heading to the town for an aperitif in one of the lively squares or narrow cobbled streets. These elegant squares, the higgledy-piggledy houses leaning against each other for comfort (and to stop them from falling down) and numerous bars and restaurants make this town a magnet for tourists, and it is a lively, thriving place all year round.

In July every village puts on a show of straw sculptures to celebrate the fertile land, the summer, the harvest — any excuse, really, for a festive event. Preparation is a closely guarded secret, and everyone who participates in putting the sculptures together is sworn to complete silence. Woe betide anyone who leaks information to the opposing teams.

Using a few props is allowed but strictly controlled and the aim is to create something that is more than 90 per cent straw and is limited to one creation per village though it may take the form of a tableau or a single item. It must be aesthetically pleasing, topical, and a bit of humour helps.

It's a fiercely fought competition. One year, one of the villages (I can't say which; I do have to live here, you know) got very ambitious and tried to create an ethereal concept (no one seems to know exactly what and those who do aren't telling) off-site. However, on the day when the team had to erect their masterpiece on the village green, disaster struck. Their creation was so huge and complex that the whole thing collapsed. The village was disqualified. As a result they refused to take part the year after.

The straw sculptures are planned for weeks in advance and, at the crack of dawn on the day that they are to take pride of place in each of the dozen or so participating villages, the committee members meet. Formed of volunteers these are the groups who have debated and argued over what form the sculpture for their village will take. They create the masterpieces and beg, steal and borrow bits and pieces to dress up their artworks; no purchases are allowed. It's considered a serious role and participants are expected to treat their assignment with appropriate sincerity.

Village squares are tidied, troughs of flowers are pruned, grass is coiffed — everything to make their tour de force stand out. In some towns, the main road is lined with tall spikes holding oil lanterns, ready to be lit when darkness falls. In the kitchens of town halls and *salles des fêtes*, enormous buckets of mussels are washed and readied to feed the visiting crowds.

One village created Asterix's town complete with houses and characters; another built an enormous windmill; there are animals, people, cars, aeroplanes. It seems that the sky's the limit when it comes to straw art.

Throughout the day a steady stream of cars will pass through normally tranquil towns. Some people are checking out the competition, others are there to sightsee during daylight hours, but they often return at night when residents train spotlights on their creations. En route visitors will collect a voting form, for this is a prestigious occasion and there is a lot of good-natured effort aimed at persuading sightseers to support this or that village's attempts.

As dusk falls, the illuminations are turned on. Lots of houses make good use of their Christmas tree lights, trailing them over fences and gate posts, rose bushes and arbours, adding a twinkling magic to the night. There are long convoys of slow cars going from village to village, enjoying the efforts that have been made. Spectators mark their voting forms and stop off for a beer, a glass of wine, to listen to music, dance, eat mussels and socialize with friends and neighbours.

The sound of people enjoying themselves can be heard going on long into the night, joined by village dogs barking and howling, not used to such hullabaloo in these quiet little enclaves.

The winning village of this illustrious contest will enjoy the kudos; the losers will grit their teeth and vow to try harder next year. The sculptures remain for several weeks, often becoming climbing frames for local kids until eventually they fall apart or are removed and recycled by farmers as animal bedding.

It seemed incredible to me then, and still does, that I could get from London to

Montreuil-sur-Mer or any one these villages in just three hours and live an utterly different and typically French lifestyle.

8

Decision Time

It was two years after we'd bought the French house that Mark's younger sister Loraine was diagnosed with cancer. She was a vibrant, funny, beautiful woman, and when she died just a year later we were devastated. It hit Mark very hard. He had always been a protective big brother: if she ever had a problem she would tell Mark and he would do his best to sort it out. She and her husband Martin had spent many weekends with us in France and they'd fallen completely in love with it and had dreams to buy a house near us one day.

One night about six months after her passing, Mark collected me from the train station after yet another long day in the office and we drove to our house in the suburbs and parked by our neat front garden, which was lined up with all the other neat front gardens. Mark switched the engine off and before I could get out of the car he turned to me and said, 'We need to talk. I want to move to France. I want us to spend some time together.'

Moving to the French house was something we'd talked about doing, but not until we were a lot older, perhaps in twenty years, but certainly not now. I worked at a merchant bank and, after eighteen years, I'd reached the level of Vice President of Operations. It sounds a lot better than it really was, as there were hundreds of VPs, but, to me, having started as a secretary and worked my way up, it meant a great deal. My role was demanding, the hours were long, I frequently worked weekends and I often needed to go to Switzerland for meetings, but I loved my job and the people I worked with. Not only that, my bosses had hinted that I would be put forward for a directorship programme. I was ecstatic. Though I was ambitious, I'd never imagined reaching the level of director. I stopped worrying about working long hours or being away from home and Mark was brilliant, supporting me wholeheartedly. He had trained as a financial advisor not long after I met him and he too had a challenging schedule. Sometimes we would only see each other for a few hours a week.

By late 2007, financial pundits were predicting a recession was on its way and it seems they were right, as soon after the gloomy announcement Mark's job had been made redundant. He took up work as a builder again — one of his many previous incarnations — and, though he didn't mind it, he told me he wanted to be working on our house, not someone else's. He wanted us to be spending more time together, not just meeting for a few hours a day. 'Life is too short to spend it working all the hours under the sun,' he said. There was a big part of me that knew he was right, but the thought of becoming a director in the bank was so tempting. We talked long into the night and I couldn't bring myself to agree with Mark's dream of changing our lives so drastically.

I was adamant. 'It's too big a risk to go to France now. We're too young and too poor. It's a crazy idea.'

When Mark told me that he would go without me, it was like being punched in the stomach. We slept in separate rooms that night and in the morning I went to work before Mark was up. I worked late and afterwards went out with my friends, staying in the pub until it closed. When I went home we had a huge row.

'Team Janine,' said Mark, as he accused me of being selfish for not even considering what he wanted us to do.

'You're mad,' I told him. How could we afford even to think about giving up our jobs?

We had twenty years to go until we reached retirement age. Although I had a house that I'd bought before I met Mark, there was a mortgage to pay off and we didn't have savings. For an entire week we either avoided each other or argued.

I couldn't sleep and my mind was in a mess. I didn't want to lose Mark and I knew that he could be very stubborn. I also knew that he had really supported me, never complaining when I worked late or away, taking care of things at home. I realized that losing his sister had had a deep impact, had made him feel vulnerable and reassess his life and our life together.

In the end it boiled down to whether my job and earning more money was more important than the man I loved. And the honest truth was that actually I loved them both, and it wasn't easy to choose. But at the back of my mind was the memory of my mum. She could have retired in her early fifties after she survived treatment for breast cancer but she kept pushing herself to keep going. 'Just six more months so I can save for a new sofa for the front room,' she'd promise, or, 'Just a few more months so I can save for a carpet for the hall.' Mum and Dad were very much 'neither a borrower nor a lender be' types: if you didn't have the money you couldn't have the goods, and credit cards were a no-no for them. For Mum, that meant that there was always something to keep her at work until she reached sixty. She wanted the house to be perfect. Mark built her an extension and a pond and the very last thing she wanted to save for was to buy her dream greenhouse. Less than a year after her retirement party at work, she was dead from cancer. She never got her greenhouse.

Mum was very bitter about not having time to enjoy the things she had worked for and spend time with her family. In her final few days, as we sat quietly in the hospice that she never went home from, she took my hand and said, 'You're just like me. You have to be careful that you don't end up just like me.'

I knew what she meant, that I was driven like her. I felt a need to prove myself and work was my outlet. That was never more evident than when Mum died and I threw myself into my job. It took my mind off the terrible loss I felt. I worked with a great bunch of people; they were more than just work colleagues, they were my friends too, and we were a close-knit group. For a long time after my mum died, being in the office felt less stressful than being out of it, where I had time to think.

As I mulled over the options I had, I knew

what my mum would say, that sometimes you have to go with your heart, you have to give a different life a chance before it was too late. I made my choice. 'Let's do it, let's go to France,' I said, and Mark hugged me tight.

We discussed what we would do to the French house, how we would make it our dream home, how I would grow tomatoes and cucumbers. We would shop at the market every week and do all the things we'd never had time for. Mark's enthusiasm for what he wanted to do to the house was infectious. He was going to extend the narrow kitchen, turn the pigsty into a gym, and make the uninhabitable upper rooms into a huge bedroom with a dressing room and en-suite bathroom.

Even though I had put my faith in this man, whom I loved, a part of me still felt as though I had gone along with *his* dream instead of my own. Working my way up the greasy pole of promotion to about-to-be-director had taken eighteen years of hard work. There was family to think of, and friends. Our children were independent by then but it would be a massive wrench not to have them come with us. There was my dad to consider too — since my mum had died I had seen him at least once every week.

Our families were supportive — all except

Dad. When I told him what we'd decided, he told me I was an idiot and tried to talk me out of it, and he almost succeeded. He had always taken his responsibilities seriously, and for him that was largely about earning the money to pay your bills, pay your mortgage, and not have to borrow. He never cared for praise; he would tap the table with his fingertips stressing, 'You can't put well done on the table.' A stubborn little bit of me still wanted to be a director and earn lots of money, but I could hear Mum's voice in my head. I felt sure that she would urge me to take a chance to live my life in a different way and to not waste my chances. Money is important and you need enough to live, of course, but did it really have to be more than enough, she would ask me if she were here.

I also didn't want to leave my father, so I asked him to come with us and offered to sell the French house and buy another with separate accommodation for him so that he would have his own space. 'Only if there's a betting shop nearby,' was his answer, but he wasn't serious. By then he was spending more time with his friends and doing voluntary work, playing bridge four times a week, and although he missed my mum, he was getting on with life. We were three hours away from him in France if anything happened, I figured, so the decision was definite: I resolved to take a risk and follow my heart.

When I resigned, my boss tried to persuade me to stay. I had been approved for a directorship programme that would complete in fifteen months' time, he said. There would be a great pay rise, a great bonus — all that I'd worked so hard for. The project I'd been working on had a year left to run and apparently I was considered essential to its completion. I thought of my mum sticking it out for a bit more money for this and that. I thought of Loraine and the chances she would never have. I thought of Mark who was so excited about us spending time together and making a new life, who would go to France without me.

I stuck to my decision, but my boss refused to accept my letter of resignation and said he would talk to me about it later in the day. When he did, I nearly fell off my chair in shock when he proposed to almost double my salary if I stayed. I told him I would think about it.

That night Mark and I talked again. By now, having decided we did both want to go to France, we were more rational and less emotional about it. We decided that the money was too good to refuse and we should spend time planning properly for a move. I never told Mark how secretly relieved I was to stay; I gracefully accepted my boss's offer.

Meanwhile, we put my house up for sale. I have to admit I was heartbroken. I'd worked so hard to buy it and hold on to it when times were hard, but we couldn't afford to do up the French house without the money from the London house. I'd bought it almost twenty years before and the value had increased substantially. When it sold almost immediately, I cried my eyes out but it meant that we had enough money to renovate in France and live on for a few years while we sorted out a way to earn an income. We moved into Mark's mum's house. She had moved out recently, having remarried, and because the rent was low it meant we could save money by living there, so it was a no-brainer.

It felt like time went by in a flash. We hardly had any opportunity to go out to France as I was working long hours to finish the project, including lots of weekends. We saved every penny we could. I walked to work instead of taking the bus, took packed lunches instead of eating in the staff canteen. We kept a spreadsheet of every penny we spent. We scrimped and scraped like a pair of crazy people.

When the project at work finished a year

later, I handed in my notice again and this time it was accepted. There were just three months to go until I made director and there was a part of me that felt sad and disappointed, but deep down I knew I was doing the right thing. My colleagues threw me a party and gave me presents to remember them by, including an envelope with a picture of a chicken and the words 'To be opened when you get to France'.

My friends took bets on how long it would be before I came back. No one, including me, could quite believe what I'd actually done or thought I would last as long as six months away from London or my job.

9

Madame Merde

For most people starting out on the path to a new life in a new home in a new country, moving-in day is exhilarating.

More than four years had passed between buying the house in France and moving there permanently, and it was certainly an emotional day, though for a rather different reason than you might expect.

It was mid-September, the sun was shining, we were filled with a mixture of excitement and anticipation, and for me an element of worry that Mark appeared not to share. For months before, while I'd been working weekends, he had been taking our belongings out to France in boxes and now we were down to the final tranche.

We towed a huge open trailer behind the car; it was filled to the brim with our possessions, ready to go on the Eurotunnel train. It attracted quite a bit of attention on the way: the UK border control guard told me he liked my armchairs and on the train people came past in a steady stream to look and comment on my belongings, from cupboards to rugs. It's amazing how cheeky people can be, talking about your precious belongings, and not always in a complimentary way (although absolutely everyone loved the old Windsor chair that had been my mum's and which would take pride of place in my French kitchen).

We drove carefully to our little village, especially going up and down the steep hills that run through the Forest of Boulogne and lead to the Seven Valleys. We reached our village and finally made our way up the little hill to our house. By now, instead of feeling excited, I was scared. I still had gnawing doubts about moving to rural France. It is very quiet. I had come to love it there and it was more than all right for the weekends and holidays, but for a whole lifetime? I entered the house prepared for the customary sickly smell of damp. I was ready for the spiders' webs, perhaps a bird or two, a feral cat, rodent droppings.

What I didn't expect was the unmistakeable smell of sewage.

The toilet was basically a boxed-off area (not unlike the coffin-like porch) in a corner off the kitchen, with a loo. A waste pipe led straight out of the wall and into a septic tank. I had never even heard of such a thing before

I'd bought this house, but without mains drainage, all the household waste goes into an enormous plastic tank buried in the ground. Bacteria do their thing and get rid of most of the contents, leaving liquid to seep through small holes and into the surrounding earth. Once in a while the whole thing has to be emptied.

Our septic tank had decided not to wait for someone to come round with all the right equipment to drain. Instead it had decided to discharge itself and was busy making friends with the garden as its repellent contents oozed out of the top of the tank from which the lid had somehow gone missing.

Any ideas of celebrating our arrival came to an abrupt halt. We had no telephone and no mobile phone signal and, besides, we didn't know who to ring. We made our way down the road to François the farmer's house and hoped someone would be able to advise us. His two dogs ran out barking and, as I've been afraid of dogs since I was a child, I stood frozen to the spot. Mark found it hilarious and, putting his arm around my shoulders, pulled me forward, assuring me that the boisterous barking and jumping up was a friendly greeting. We had more pressing concerns, anyway.

François invited us into the kitchen to tell

our tale of woe. The kitchen was tiny and yellow. (Apparently yellow is one of the most popular colours for kitchens in France, inspired by Monet's kitchen at Giverny.) Somehow he had managed to cram in a sink, cupboards, a table and chairs in a space that would fit into a Renault van. On the work surface was a huge hock of ham; flies buzzed around it and on it, and I sat watching them, mesmerized. Mark jabbed me with his elbow as François came over with a small cup of black liquid he called coffee. I can honestly say it was the first time I had ever drunk mud, as I am sure that is what it really was. François had seen me staring at the ham and mistook my amazement for desire. He whipped out his pocketknife and offered to cut me off a lump. As he lunged towards the pink meat with the tip of his blade, the flies buzzed manically.

'Non, merci,' I assured him with all the emphasis I could muster without sounding too hysterical.

He shrugged and cut himself a hunk and popped it in his mouth. He listened to us explain the problem with the tank and said, 'No problem. I, François, shall arrive later and sort it out for you. I have to go and feed the cows now but I will come back before dinner.'

Our new life was only a couple of hours old and I was already starting to feel queasy about it. Flies, merde, dogs — London life it definitely was not.

We spent the afternoon dragging boxes and furniture into the house while trying not to breathe in the noxious smell that filled the air. We made sure to put beer in the fridge for when François came. We'd learned enough by now to know that when our neighbours visited, they were as disgusted by our coffee as we were by theirs.

We knew when François had arrived, since he drove his full-sized tractor straight into our garden and past the kitchen window, creating huge craters in the vegetable beds Mark had spent the summer weekends preparing. Behind the tractor was an enormous silver cylinder-shaped storage tank of the sort you usually see carrying milk or oil.

François was accompanied by his young assistant, Gaetar.

I didn't need to show either of them where the septic tank was. François informed me that it had been at least seven years since it had been emptied and he knew this since he himself had been the one to empty it. Seven years. It doesn't bear thinking about.

Gaetar proceeded to unwind a massive

hosepipe and pull it towards the septic tank. He and François bickered constantly while they worked. I watched apprehensively from the back door as they pushed the end of the pipe into the opening of the septic tank.

Gaetar climbed into the tractor, François wandered over to the back door to drink a bottle of Page 24, the local beer known in these parts as 'the blonde who dominates', with Mark and Jean-Claude, who had just arrived. He has an uncanny knack of knowing when there's a bottle of beer about and appears as if from nowhere.

A low hum, building up to a loud mechanical whir, emerged from the tank as Gaetar activated the button to empty the septic tank. Except he didn't.

Instead of pushing the button to suck, he pushed expel.

Rather than the contents of our septic tank being discreetly drawn into the tank, everything started to spread over the garden, and into the craters the tractor had dug.

François cursed and screamed at Gaetar. 'Arrêtez-vous, stop, stop . . . you imbecile,' or words to that effect.

Gaetar swore, François swore, reluctantly put his beer down and ran to the tractor, the pair of them shouting and screaming at each other.

'That Gaetar,' said Jean-Claude, 'is remarkably idiotic sometimes. I don't know how François puts up with it. I think this might be *la goutte d'eau qui fait déborder le vase.*'

'The drop of water that makes the vase overflow?' said Mark translating it literally from his pocket French — English dictionary.

'It means the final straw that breaks the camel's back,' I said. When I told Jean-Claude that that's how we say it in English he looked at me as if I was possibly madder than Gaetar, and turned back to watch the farce, taking pictures on his phone, presumably to show to his friends later.

By now several neighbours had come into the garden to see what was going on. The pandemonium of Gaetar and François was echoing around the valley. I was panicking and almost in tears. Mark, always sane and sensible, started handing out beers.

Eventually, the right buttons were pushed, the job was done and we were left with, I think it is fair to say, quite a bit of hosing down to do. François and Gaetar refused to take any payment for resolving our problem. 'We are neighbours,' said François. 'It's only right to help each other out.'

As the sun set on that September night, we stood in the kitchen with our new neighbours, drinking beer and watching as

90

François made his way round our garden, being nosy and checking the apple trees. From time to time he would pull one of the not-yet-ready fruits off a branch and take a bite.

'*Miam*, delicious fruit,' he said. 'You can grow anything in this garden, you know. The old lady up the top of the hill only got a flushing toilet about two years ago; before that she used to go in the cow shed. I reckon, being down the hill, you've got the best soil in town.'

Later Jean-Claude told me that that was when the villagers nicknamed me 'Madame Merde'.

10

The art of small steps

Our house is a long, low building. Once an animal barn, it was extended over a lengthy period. A single room built from chunky lumps of flint stone and oak beams had been the original structure perhaps four hundred years ago, although only one wall remains. Subsequent owners added rooms made from concrete blocks, slabs of chalk, sheets of corrugated metal, wood and even a bit of old plastic fencing. It was not, by any stretch of the imagination, a feast for the eyes.

Some rooms had impressively solid ceiling beams of ancient oak; some rooms were painted lurid yellow or were lined with pine boards, turned orange by time. Some floors were concrete; others were plain earth left that way for decades, perhaps centuries. You might think that sounds quite romantic. I assure you it is not, especially when you have to dig out some of that old dirt to lay foundations for a proper floor.

A previous owner with no sense of style had created the upper floor, reached by the spiral hobbit staircase. Somebody had apparently been sleeping up there. We know this because the previous occupant left a rusty old bed, and a piece of cotton material that formed a minuscule curtain pegged on to a line of string across the only, tiny, window. It was dark upstairs; it was a place of spiders' webs and strange smells, muffled scratching, squeaks and draughts. When it rained, water came in liberally, and there were patches of mould on the boarded floor, which bounced horribly when walked upon.

It's odd how you don't notice quite how bad things are when you don't have them under your nose all the time. We had already decided to do all of the work ourselves, mainly because we couldn't afford to pay anyone else but also because we wanted to create something that truly represented us. If you ask me now would we do it again, I'm not sure I would say yes.

Our first job was to find storage for the boxes containing all our belongings. Putting them upstairs seemed the obvious choice and that's when we discovered yet another problem. A mezzanine floor had been created in the high roof space, just plain boards set on top of a scaffold of wooden planks, like an enormous shelf. We hadn't really taken much notice of it before; we just assumed it was a storage area and because it was so dark we had ignored it. We knew it had to come down, as it was neither safe nor useful stuck 2 metres up in the air. We climbed a ladder to see what was up there only to discover that it had been covered with about 30 centimetres of pinky-brown clay-like material with bits of straw in it. It was also slathered over much of the walls upstairs.

'Ah yes,' said Jean-Claude when we asked him about it — he had become our go-to Frenchman — 'some country folk used to apply a layer of straw and mud to fill in gaps in the walls and floors. It keeps the wind and cold out and adds a layer of insulation. Smells disgusting.'

What it also adds is a whole lot of work you didn't know you had to do before you could even store boxes.

It took days to pull the floor down and shovel all that dried mud out of the window. We wore masks and at the end of each day, when we took them off, we could easily have auditioned for the part of Baloo the bear in *The Jungle Book*. When it was finally done and we had cleared out all of the rubbish, we found we had one very long room upstairs that could be made into three bedrooms and two bathrooms, but at that stage we were a considerable way from actually creating any living space. We stored the boxes that contained the remnants of our London life up there. One day, when Mark fell up those narrow, dangerous spiral stairs and cut his head open, causing him to look like a human money box, he ripped them out in a temper and access was by ladder only, and that's how it stayed for two years.

It started to dawn on us just how much work there was to do. There were thirty-seven windows and thirteen doors that needed replacing and, though we didn't know it then, more than 100 tonnes of concrete would be mixed by the time we were finished. To all intents and purposes we aimed to build an entirely new house within the old one.

The first month went by in a whirl of mud removal and cleaning. The weather was fine and the fact that I had no oven but had to cook on a barbecue in the garden was not a problem. We'd become accustomed to making do in France. We had no television, no phone and no internet; our mobile phones could only be used if we left the bottom of the bowl that is the valley in which our village sits. A month can easily be used up — it's little more than a lengthy holiday and we worked long days.

In mid-October, it started to get colder. We thought about heating. But we didn't get much further than that. There was one fire in the whole house, an ugly old wood stove in a corner of the front room with its very chilly tiled floor — but it was big. Surely, we reasoned, the people living here before us thought it was sufficient, so it must be fine. The cold Christmases we had spent here had become a distant memory and we convinced ourselves the problem was just because we weren't there permanently and so the fire never had sufficient time to build up a good blaze for a long period.

By then I was starting to really miss my friends and family. I wanted to get the internet and phone sorted out so that I could at least communicate. We discovered that this required us to go in person to an Orange Telecom shop (our nearest one is an hour's drive) to complete the forms. When we got there they informed us we needed to come back with a utility bill and various other bits of paper. We returned a week later, signed up and were told we should have a phone line by Christmas. I protested that we wanted it sooner and was dismissed with a Gallic shrug. Sometimes the shrug means 'I wish I could help' or 'that's the way it is', sometimes it means 'whatever' or 'talk to the hand'.

By mid-November it was bitterly cold. The condensation that ran down the inside of the windows in our bedroom turned to ice on its journey — at least it prevented the pool of dirty water that usually collected on the windowsill. A glass of water left at the side of the bed had a fine layer of ice crystals by the morning. The water in the pipes was glacial. My feelings for life in France followed suit.

Our fire was useless and ate through our wood stock at an alarming rate. By now all the bigger stores that sold wood had run out in the cold spell and we had no idea where to get more from.

We bought a couple of oil heaters and at night would sit, each with a heater at our side, facing the beautifully bright but horribly hopeless wood fire, wearing coats, hats, gloves and scarves, watching a DVD or trying to read a book, which wasn't easy as you had to keep removing gloves to turn the pages.

During the day we were still managing to work on the house, which kept my mind occupied; at night I would start to daydream about going back to London. When it reached a highly unusual — 20 degrees Celsius I was ready to give up. I sat in the kitchen, shivering and wondering what on earth had made me think I was cut out for country life — I was a city girl, and I wanted to be back in a city, in a warm office in the day, and a warm house at night. I wanted to have a good old moan with one of my friends; I was desperately missing them. It was cold and damp; we woke up every morning coughing and feeling unwell.

It was about then that we both realized that we didn't know each other as well as we thought. We had been together for several years, but not twenty-four hours a day, seven days a week, as we were now. It was tough. Our flaws and foibles were revealed. I had had no idea that Mark was so bossy. He had had no idea *I* was so bossy. There was a power struggle; it was at times subconscious and at others as clear as day. We were freezing. We argued. We disagreed.

I like order when it comes to planning, and graphs and maps of what needs to be done. Mark likes to rush in and just *do*.

I knew Mark had a quick temper, but the frustrations of learning a new language, the huge project and the cold weather fuelled his bad moods more than I'd ever seen before. The day all the pipes in the house froze so that we had no water at all, it was like opening a gate of fury. We had an almighty row, both admitting that we were not happy. We were pulling apart. We'd been in France nine weeks and I felt as though I had made an enormous mistake. I wanted to go home. Back to the UK.

I retreated to the greenhouse where, feeling

sorry for myself, I sat shivering (it still wasn't warm despite the winter sun) and crying. I wasn't comfortable driving on the wrong side of the road or I would have taken the car and driven back to the UK there and then. I had made some friends in France but none I felt relaxed enough to talk to about how I felt. I could walk up the hill to call a friend in the UK on my mobile phone, but they were all at work. Dad would tell me I was whining. I cried some more.

Then I wrote out a list of what I would need to do if I was to give up and go home:

1. Go back to the bank or get a new job.
2. Find somewhere to live, maybe stay with Dad.
3. Get a car.
4. Get a divorce. Probably.

Why had I done this? Over and over again I wondered how I would tell everyone that I'd given up after such little effort. I sat in the greenhouse for two hours, my fingers frozen, my nose running and my eyes red with crying. I wanted Mark to come and find me, say sorry and tell me it would all be fine. He didn't. In the end, when it started to get dark and I could hardly feel my toes because they were so cold, I went back to the house.

'I want to go home,' I told Mark. 'I hate it here. It's cold and dirty. I have no friends. I hate it.'

'Okay,' he replied and went to bed, where at least it was warm under the duvet. I slept on the sofa, covered in coats and blankets, feeling like a failure and wondering if 'okay' meant go back on your own or let's go back together.

Once again Jean-Claude came to the rescue. He regularly stops by for a chat and a beer, though no matter what time of the day it is he won't drink our coffee, and, as for tea, you might think he had been offered a pint of Paraquat the way he reacted when once I offered it to him.

He came by on the morning after the row to find us bundled up in blankets but still breathing frost patterns in the kitchen and barely on speaking terms, considering giving it all up and returning to the UK. He is generous in nature and very practical and suggested his friend Patrice could help with the wood.

'What we really need is a new fire,' we said.

'No problem.' (This is Jean-Claude's answer to everything.) 'My friend fits fires and I'll ask him to sort you out as a priority.'

At that stage we were somewhat naïve about the ways of French workmen and artisans.

Mark and I kissed and made up. I said sorry, he said sorry. We assured each other we would make it work. Filled with hope, I tore up my list, pulled my woollen scarf tighter and believed that all would be well. Soon. After all, the word priority had been used.

The wood came the next week. Without alerting us to his arrival, Patrice drove his huge tractor into the garden and dumped 10 tonnes of logs on the grass. It took us two days to stack them but we didn't care: we were ecstatic. So much wood — we thought it would last us a good long while with our new fire when it arrived. And that is a lesson for all expats in France — relish the moment. The wood wasn't even enough to see us through one winter: we had to get another load in by March, when it was still cold, and we were still using our futile fire.

We didn't know then that some things take longer than you might expect. Much longer. In fact, they may never happen at all. We opened a bottle of wine and we opened up to each other. Mark needed to express himself; I needed to not take things personally. We both needed to accept each other's idiosyncrasies. I created a project plan that showed the priority jobs and dependencies and Mark agreed that clarifying the jobs we needed to do was helpful. When he needed to vent his frustrations, I tried to let him be until he worked it out.

As for the new fire, every month for a very long time, Jean-Claude told us his friend would come to fit it. We bought the fire, we bought the bits. We waited. The fantasy fire fitter never arrived. We learned to fit it ourselves before the end of the next year rather than face another frozen winter in the house.

That first Christmas of our new lives was celebrated with an ice cold glass of champagne that hadn't needed to be chilled in the fridge — we just left the bottle on the kitchen table and enjoyed it with barbecued turkey legs and microwaved potatoes.

Shortly after Christmas we were joined by a cat. I had never had a pet as a child, never wanted one as an adult and hadn't ever considered getting one in France. But that all changed when we went to shop in the hypermarket in the ancient port town of Boulogne-sur-Mer, and ended up going home with more than we bargained for.

We were sitting with Mark's stepfather Dave and mum Sylvia in a restaurant in the commercial shopping area, a place where lots of stray cats congregate around the car parks and scavenge for food. Sylvia was grimacing at the Frenchman on the table next to us who was relishing every mouthful of his steak tartare. 'It's raw mincemeat,' she whispered dramatically, in a tone of utter horror. Suddenly, she gasped out loud. Bloody hell, I thought, they must have brought the snails out. But no, she said she could see a tiny kitten being attacked by a bigger cat in the car park of the restaurant — we all looked, nothing there. Mark replenished her wine glass and we carried on, thinking no more of it.

When we got to our car on leaving the restaurant, Mark leaned down and from behind one of the wheels pulled out a kitten. The animal was covered in blood, its nose was all but hanging off and it didn't move; it just lay there pathetically. We couldn't leave it and although we knew nothing about cats we decided to take it home and at least let the poor creature have a last night in safety.

On the way home we stopped at the vets to buy kitten food, milk and a pipette, which we used to squirt milk straight into the little thing's mouth. We put the kitten in a cardboard box with a blanket, a bowl of water and some newspaper and left it in the hall when we went to bed. We really didn't think it would pull through, as it was in such a bad way.

I got up early in the morning and was

shocked to find the kitten gone. But not far: it had escaped from the box and was now cavorting happily round the kitchen, diving under cupboards and mewing and playing. It was a boy and we named him Winston after Winston Churchill. A white kitten with black markings on his head and in the shape of wings on his back, he was adorable. He had bright blue eyes and the vet we took him to said he was probably only four weeks old. Over time his injuries healed, he ate more and more and is now the biggest cat in the village.

Winston is not a friendly cat; he is obsessive and highly strung, he doesn't like people, is scared of loud noises and won't come in if he hears music being played or there is anyone other than us in the house. He is very affectionate with me, though, and is very talkative with a large repertoire of mews and chirrups. He also likes nothing more than to dig up whatever I have just planted in the vegetable patch.

Winston's arrival was the start of a slippery animal slide. We shopped each week in Boulogne and bought his kitten food in a pet shop there. Almost three months after we had found Winston, Mark remarked that there was a dog in one of the glass cages in the pet shop that he was sure had been there for at least eight weeks. It was a sorry-looking tiny russet-coloured creature. The label on the cage said Pinscher and the price had been slashed. Mark asked a member of staff if he could get the dog out of its cage to have a look. I had always been afraid of dogs but this one's big, sad brown eyes melted my objections and the wag of his feeble tail broke my heart. Mark told me that he thought the dog would likely be put down if it weren't sold soon.

'I've always wanted a Doberman Pinscher,' he said looking into my eyes. What could I say, the last time I'd done it to him I bought a house. We left carrying a dog we called Churchill, who turned out not to be a Doberman at all but a German Pinscher.

Churchill does not think he is a dog. We should have called him Pinocchio, since he feels he is a real boy and wishes to get involved with whatever we are doing. He also does not like to be alone. This was fine when he was with us during the day, but at night in his own bed in another room, he howled endlessly.

A month later he was joined by the dog that had been in the glass cage with him. She was labelled a spaniel and her price had also been slashed. Like Churchill it seemed she did not appeal to any of the customers. The day we got her, Churchill stopped crying at night and the pair have been inseparable ever since. The pet shop closed shortly after, which was a huge relief or we may have ended up with a dozen sorrowful-looking dogs.

We called the new dog Ella Fitzgerald after one of our favourite singers. A few months after we took her home it became obvious that she wasn't a spaniel at all, despite what it said on her registration forms. The sweet puppy we brought home was already way too big for a spaniel. She has shaggy dark golden hair, white paws like little boots, a white patch on her chest and huge brown eyes that she blinks at you to communicate. She is in fact a large mutt that is mostly German Shepherd and she is neurotic to the point of lunacy at times. I have a few phobias — spiders, heights, flying, dentists — but Ella has way more. She doesn't like remote controls: we have to hide them or she will eat them. She doesn't like fence posts and will happily chew them until it looks as if giant chipmunks have been busy in the garden. She hates noisy children, strangers, strange noises, other dogs, cats that aren't ours and chickens. In fact, her dislikes are far too long to list. She will merrily pull nails out of the wall and chew doors; once she ate a leather sofa. Churchill, her partner in crime, dances around adoringly while she misbehaves and then alerts us to her misdeeds by barking insistently — afterwards, of course. She is the most affectionate dog and when she turns her big brown eyes on me I find it hard to tell her off.

Work carried on with the house and the cat and the two dogs lived with us among bags of cement powder, tubs of paint, sheets of plasterboard and a thousand tools.

11

The best-laid plans of mice and men

We got through that first winter by keeping the fire going and wearing two sets of clothing until spring finally came. Plants pushed through the frozen soil and burst into flower, we woke to the sound of birdsong, and it was warm enough to carry on working without stuffing our cold fingers into gloves that slowed us down.

We'd read enough books about living in France to know that we needed to make sure we didn't fall foul of administrative requirements when it came to renovating. It feels like every article I've ever read about expat life includes a reference to a benevolent mayor who goes out of his or her way to help the newcomers settle in to their new life.

This is not one of those stories.

The mayor is an important figure in France as the position wields quite a lot of power. There are around 36,700 mayors, almost enough to fill the O_2 Arena twice over. Mayors are like little kings of the communes they represent, despite the fact that some 80 per cent of the mayoral municipalities have fewer than a thousand residents. My own village, for example, has a mayor. There are 142 inhabitants in the village, including second home owners. The next village along also has a mayor — for 180 people — and so on. When you're a mayor, size is important, but not essential. Our mayor recently commissioned a new road through the village after the old one started to disintegrate from the combination of the many tractors that use it and a couple of harsh winters. Some in the village say that the real reason the road was commissioned was that the old road was too narrow for the mayor's new tractor. My little bit of road, which is in a U-shape annex off the main road, was left untouched. Everyone else got new drives, fences, kerbs and a spruce up. The cost of this smart new thoroughfare, around a mile long, was about half a million euros. We were astonished. And worried that the bill would be shared among the 142 people in the village (though this does include children who would presumably have to be subsidized). We haven't heard anything yet, but this being France, we still occasionally wake up in the middle of the night after dreams of a road bill that will ruin us.

When it comes to bureaucracy, it often

feels like the more complicated it is, the better the French like it. Indeed, France could win an Olympic gold medal for creating complicated, long drawn-out administrative processes.

We decided that we wanted to extend the kitchen. It's a long, narrow room with three doors and featured a big window that took up most of the wall overlooking the garden, which made me fall in love with the house in the first place. With that many openings there wasn't much wall left for cupboards. We asked our French neighbours if they would be happy for us to add a small room of about 15 square metres on to the back of the house to make the kitchen bigger. Not that they could see anything in our garden as it is encircled by tall hedges, but it seemed the right thing to do. No problem, they said. We also want to put roof windows in the front of the house, we told them. We can't see out of them but we need more light, we explained. Again, no problem.

I'd done my homework: I knew from my books that we simply needed to inform the mayor what we wanted to do, get permission and submit drawings and details and fill in a form or two. It seemed so easy! Well, it is if you believed the books and didn't take into account the constant tweaking of rules by various administrative departments, which seem to operate to different procedures in different areas.

Mark measured up, drew pictures, took photographs and created diagrams to scale. We filled in forms and took everything to the town hall to show to the mayor.

He got another form out, confirmed he had seen our drawings and the request to amend our house. With a flurry he twirled his moustache and gave the request the stamp of approval.

We were stunned. Everyone always complained about how hard it was to get planning permission in France. It was easy. We smiled and thanked the mayor and shook his hand vigorously and enthusiastically.

We collected our paperwork. We made for the door.

'Ahem.' We stopped in our tracks as the mayor's secretary shook her pen in our direction. Yes, he does have a secretary, even though the town hall is only open for four hours a week in the winter and six hours a week in the summer.

I knew it. I knew it had gone too well. I waited for the words that would burst my planning ecstasy bubble.

'I need to take copies,' said the secretary.

We trundled over, all smiles. Ah, that's not

so bad. The photocopies were made, slowly. We didn't care; we had permission.

The secretary came over and gave us the paperwork and the form back. The form that gave us permission.

'You need to take this to the Deh Deh Err,' she said.

'Pardon?'

'The Deh Deh Err in Montreuil.'

She wrote it down: DDE.

We had no idea what she was talking about but we smiled sweetly, thanked her for her help and left.

It turned out that it wasn't as simple as just getting the mayor to sign off on your plans. We were required to get further permission from the official planning department in the nearest main town.

We went to the DDE (Directions Départmentales de l'Equipment), the equivalent of a town planning department, and discussed the paperwork with an administrator, who nodded and smiled at us. We took this to be a good sign. We left a box load of notes, photos, forms and drawings as required and prepared to receive the go-ahead.

We went back to the DDE office several times over the course of the following months to ask if permission would be forthcoming. We submitted more paperwork on a number of occasions as they asked for an additional photo or an extra measurement, this, that and the other. There seemed to be no end to the number of requests, and in despair I went to the mayor to ask for help.

'It's just a question of waiting,' he said philosophically, with a typically Gallic shrug.

Two weeks later I met his secretary at the market and we stopped to chat. I told her that the waiting for permission was getting me down — it had been almost a year by now — and she advised me to get an architect to submit the request. Even though we didn't need to according to the regulations, she said she thought it would help. I was at my wits' end and paid an architect to redraw the paperwork and submit everything.

It was then that we discovered that the *cadastre*, the land registry document that shows the plot of our land and the buildings on it, bore no relation whatsoever to the building plans we had submitted. The architect called within days to say that she had heard from the DDE and they had rejected our permit because it didn't make sense because the drawings of our current building did not match their records.

It turned out that the *notaire* had not checked any of the cadastral plans when we bought the house. The paperwork in the government registry showed a building of six rooms. We had bought a building with eleven rooms and a considerably bigger footprint. At no point did anyone ever mention it to us at the DDE, but one phone call from the architect sorted it out. One week later we had our permits.

It appeared that since the last updated record of our house in the early 1970s, successive owners had added more and more rooms to the building but no one had ever mentioned it or thought to update the records.

'Why bother?' said Jean-Claude when we told him about it. 'No one ever tells the authorities what they are doing unless they absolutely have to. You British are so odd with your rules.'

I thought about how odd people were when a short while later we discovered the strange fact that we lived in the land of the giants.

Giants have been around for centuries in these parts — huge wicker models that it is said represented biblical figures in the old days, but which over time have come to represent local heroes or animals, more folklore than Bible.

Giants have their own 'lifestyle': from time to time they get together with giants from neighbouring towns. Over the course of decades giants may marry, die and even have children.

In Grand-Fort-Philippe (on the coast at Gravelines) one Saturday, a giant known as La Matelote was due to give birth, and the whole town turned out in celebration.

Local TV film crews and journalists arrived, ready to record this historic birth. Bands played, giants from towns and villages all around arrived to join in the fun and the crowd was jubilant.

The mayor of Gravelines stood on a makeshift podium set up outside the town's museum, surrounded by local celebrities and dignitaries; Miss Grand-Fort-Philippe, the resident beauty queen, greeted the crowds; speeches were made. It was all very formal. Baton twirlers whirled to crazy hyper dance music, their sticks lifted away by the breeze that came in off the English Channel, their glittery eye shadow flashing in the sun.

The mayor welcomed the 'midwife' to the stage. Dressed in her nurse's uniform, she took the microphone and announced, 'The baby is born . . . it is a little girl and both mother and baby are well. The baby weighs thirty kilograms and she is two metres thirty-two centimetres tall. Her mother, La Matelote, is very happy with her family of four children — two boys and now two girls.'

As Mark and I shared a look of utter bemusement, a mighty cheer went up at the news. Then there was a moment of hush. La Matelote was carried out into the crowd by several strong lads; her makeup was immaculate and she looked serene and proud, as befitted a new mother. The crowd cheered again.

Then came the baby. Dressed in a white christening gown, she was the length of a very tall man, her blonde hair was plaited and she wore makeup. She was carried over our heads, up to the podium where a priest stood waiting to conduct a blessing. He welcomed Soeur (her given name) to the family of Grand-Fort-Philippe, and rejoiced that the baby was the image of her mother and asked God to bring her joy. A giant godfather and giant godmother stepped forward to meet their new giant godchild.

Everyone applauded, the priest scattered holy water over them and it was time to parade and show Soeur her new home. The dancers and band marched off; the crowds followed, the giants twirling in among them. At the town hall a formal baptism was performed, sweets were distributed to the children, another parade took place and then a glass of wine was offered to toast the baby. The occasion was half serious and half tongue in cheek.

It will be many years before a new giant is born and one day Soeur will marry and have children of her own, and the traditions will live on.

Local celebrations like that make me realize just how far apart the British and French are in terms of daily life, and sometimes I truly feel like a fish out of water. Like the day we went fishing with friends. Jean-Claude was there with his wife Bernadette and her sister Josianne, the deputy mayor of our village and several of his cronies and Carine and Dominique, Belgians who spend as much time as they can at their holiday home in the village.

'Just a fun afternoon,' said Bernadette. 'We'll have a picnic, bring something to share.'

Now, where I'm from, a picnic means sandwiches or a pork pie and a packet of crisps. In France, however, as I now know but didn't then, a picnic is a chance to show off your culinary skills with quiches and tarts, scrumptious salads, and home-made cakes and sweets.

As my neighbours laid their offerings out on a table we had set up under a tall leafy tree next to a trout lake on a sunny day, I gulped at the marvellous array of delicious food.

Then I took out my corned beef sandwiches, wrapped in foil. Everyone was watching.

'What are they?' asked Josianne curiously, and not unkindly. She is famous in these parts for her duck à l'orange.

I explained that we like beef in a tin. I was fairly sure that this would make my French friend recoil in horror.

'Ah! Bully beef,' said Jean-Claude, smiling. 'I love the bully beef.'

To my amazement, they all loved the 'bully beef' and everyone wanted to swap with us. Mark and I enjoyed goats' cheese and fresh herbs in a tart with melt in your mouth pastry; we savoured cold chicken cooked to perfection with a sprinkling of rosemary and thyme; we fell in love with croissants filled with delicate smoked salmon.

Our friends chomped on doorstep sandwiches of corned beef with pickle.

After lunch there was a serious attempt at catching trout. With Belgian, British and French honour at stake, it was all hands to the line to catch the biggest haul of the day. The shallow lake was beautifully clear, you could see the vibrant green plants waving gently on the bottom and lazy trout swimming just below the surface; dragonflies buzzed overhead and birds tweeted. All around the lake, groups of friends and families were enjoying picnics and barbecues, a typical sunny afternoon pastime in this area.

Jean-Claude had been boasting for several weeks beforehand that he was the best fisherman around, so when the catch was counted at the end of the day it was a huge surprise to discover that, along with the British contingent (Mark and me), Jean-Claude had nul points. The Belgians had the biggest catch and hosted the entire group at a barbecue at their home in the village. Jean-Claude was mercilessly teased by everyone. He put it down to the full moon, which he often blames when anything goes wrong.

When you are up to your neck in plaster and concrete, it is a great comfort to know that there is a wonderful life to be discovered outside the walls. It kept us going.

12

Village life

The transition from the gargantuan metropolis that is London to the rural countryside of northern France revealed plenty of differences. Apart from desperately missing my friends and family, a few issues popped up that I never expected, such as the problem of finding a hairdresser.

A few years ago a wild pig weighing 63 kilos managed to get into a shopping centre in Nancy, north-east France, and went crazy. It blundered its way into a hairdressing salon and smashed the place to pieces before being tranquillized. Part of me does have sympathy for the pig, as going to the hairdresser in France can be a frustrating and sometimes disastrous event. Every French hairdresser I have met seems to believe their customers are incapable of understanding what they want. You might ask for a trim and come out with a full crop. You might ask for blonde highlights and end up ginger. Both of these things have happened to me.

In a remarkably trendy-looking salon in a

small rural town, I was fooled by the Chanel-style black and white headshots in the window. I made an appointment and asked for a trim of 'no more than two centimetres' and a few blonde highlights. I knew something was wrong when I felt the scissors close to my neck, but there was no mirror to check in — I faced a blank wall. The hairdresser completed her masterpiece behind my back then revealed it to me by bringing a mirror on wheels into view. She clapped her hands with joy as I feebly mumbled 'wow' when I caught sight of my orange, very short hair.

'She said waou,' the hairdresser announced with pride to the other ladies in the room, spinning my chair round so they could all admire her handiwork. It was only then that I noticed that they all had the same short haircut that I now had.

She bent and kissed me on both cheeks and told me she knew we would be best friends. I looked at her in abject misery and wondered how long it would take to grow out. When I got home Mark stared for several minutes and, I must say, in fairness to the hairdresser, it is the first time he has ever noticed that I have had my hair done.

It's not only the hairdresser who kisses me. French people are kissing mad. They don't, on the whole, like to hug. My French friend Benedicte, who works in PR in Paris, says she finds it extremely odd that we wish to press our bodies together, wrap our arms round each other and stand there like that. Even now that I am used to all the lips to cheek stuff, when I am on a commuter train in the morning and people get in the carriage and start kissing it reminds me how French and British attitudes can be poles apart. Even more so when I am in a French office for a meeting and see people arriving for work and kissing each other. I do believe that knowing I might have had to kiss some of my former colleagues would have made me quit my job. My French friends find that notion very odd — even if they don't particularly like someone they have no problem kissing them. I haven't yet managed to successfully translate 'I would rather boil my own head than kiss my old boss' into French.

Over time, I've come to accept this habit, but I am in awe of the stamina required when it comes to an event involving many people.

The town of Douriez is close to the border with the department of Picardy. It's a place with a grand church and not much else, through which the River Authie runs gently and steadily on its way to the English Channel. It was there that I witnessed a kissing session that lasted for hours. There is not much that lures people to Douriez, though it is a pretty enough town, but with no shops, the only real draw is the *estaminet*, a local bistro-style restaurant/bar/general meeting place where you can eat or drink (and sometimes dance). It is run by Monsieur Vasseur, a retired butcher from Montreuil-sur-Mer who is famous for his sausages. On certain Fridays throughout the year he roasts a suckling pig on an open fire, there is live entertainment of the traditional kind, and the tables are filled with locals who come to enjoy this true taste of yesteryear. Sprightly and spruce, white-haired and somewhere in his seventies, Chef Vasseur will come out from the kitchen in his apron to say hello and shake hands with his happy customers. His daughter, who manages the wait staff, always tells him off for getting in the way and slowing service down. He takes no notice and the customers adore him.

One cold, dark Friday night, we drove across the plains of the Authie Valley to enjoy the famous hog roast. Several tables had been pushed together at the back of the restaurant, ready for a party. Large pieces of slate sit on the ceiling beams, showing the menu du jour — traditional meaty dishes like *pieds de cochon grillés* (grilled pigs' trotters) and *fondant de noix de joue de porc* (pigs' cheeks, to you and me). Myriad quirky artefacts hang from the walls and ceiling — old metal coffee pots, milk urns, dried hops, top hats, old signs, bottles, and jugs of all shapes colours and sizes. It makes you feel as though you are in the home of a local with an outrageous and eccentric taste for vintage.

We were warmly welcomed into the restaurant, where the *cochon de lait* was in situ in the enormous fireplace. At the bar were the three drivers of the three tractors parked outside by a sign that promised a night of accordéon, suckling pig and *tête de veau* (boiled calf's head). The men were enjoying a Friday night glass of robust vin rouge before going home after a long day of working in the fields. Otherwise the place was empty as, at 7.30 p.m., we were early by French standards.

We were seated close to the fire, where we started to melt almost immediately, but where we also had a great view of the restaurant as we sat sipping a Kir pétillant, a French apéritif of blackcurrant cassis and sparkling wine. Mix the cassis with champagne and you have a Kir royale, and with red wine, a Kir communard, named after the blood red flag of the Communards, revolutionaries in Paris in the late 1800s. You've got to love French ingenuity for getting mileage out of something, haven't you.

After an hour or so, people started to drift in and fill the seats. At the back of the restaurant where the party table was, the first two people to arrive were joined by another two; they swapped kisses, three of them, left, right, left. A group of four arrived; they made their way round the table, three more kisses per person. Then another couple, and another. It was fascinating to watch. Non-French people might shake hands across the table and order a beer or two while waiting. It wasn't like that here. Everyone waited until the whole party had arrived before ordering even so much as a glass of water. There were twenty-four chairs round that table. I began to pity the last person to get there, who would probably have chapped lips by the end of it all. I was coming to think the restaurant would close before they could eat when finally they were all seated, and surely by now they had worked up a thirst and must be gasping. We ourselves had got through our starters, main course and were awaiting our desserts.

The kissing custom extends to every aspect of life here, including when you go to the supermarket, where the checkout person will think nothing of kissing a customer and then having a chat as if they were just meeting somewhere privately without a line of people waiting to pay for their goods. It wouldn't matter if Gérard Depardieu was in the queue, late for an awards ceremony, or if the President of France had popped in for a bottle of milk and had to meet the British Queen in five minutes' time — everyone must wait for this important social ritual. Amazingly, it never seems to bother the French, but you can spot the expats a mile off, faces incredulous at the delay caused by interaction with customers by people who should be working.

I've grown to really appreciate these interludes, when I am next in the queue and can eavesdrop with impunity: it's an opportunity to learn what's going on in the village.

Learning the language, on the other hand, definitely wasn't as easy as we'd hoped. Mark knew hardly any French at all but I thought I would pick it up really easily. I'd studied French at school until I was sixteen. I spent many holidays in France, visited Paris on a regular basis and worked in Geneva where everyone spoke French. So it was a bit of a shock to discover that in our village they have a very strong accent and sometimes speak a different kind of French, for this is the land of the Ch'tis.

You might not have heard the term Ch'ti, but if you visit northern France, even if you just drive through, it's highly likely you'll come across this word in shops, on car stickers or in restaurants. It's a slang term that describes a native of northern France, a contraction of the term Ch'timi, and was an expression invented during the First World War by French soldiers to label their peers from northern France because, in the local dialect, the pronouns *toi* and *moi* were *ti* and *mi*.

Some of my neighbours find my bewilderment at the use of different words for different things highly entertaining. Jean-Claude told me that I should ask Thierry if I could have a sit on his bidet and then laughed uproariously as he explained that bidet is Ch'ti for *cheval* (horse). He said he merely thought I might like to go horse riding.

When we first came to France we had an English neighbour called Mrs Smith. I never knew her first name — she was one of those old school types who don't like to be too familiar. I very much doubt that she embraced the whole kissing thing. She did, however, speak impeccable French and knew the local dialect very well. She gave me a Ch'ti dictionary and taught me a few words to use in everyday conversations, which helped a lot, like *cayelle* (chaise/chair) and *boutelle de pinard (bonteille de vin rouge/*bottle of red wine). Unfortunately, after we'd been here just a few months, her advancing years meant that living alone, even with the help of friends and neighbours to go shopping for her or chop wood, got too much and she left to live with her daughter in the Loire. We became the only Brits in the village and had to learn the language for ourselves.

13

In which life will never be the same again

Almost six months after we left England for France, I was back in the UK.

My dad had had a heart attack not long before I left but he had recovered well and was soon back to his normal self — smoking, drinking, spending hours in the betting shop, going to the dog races, dancing round the front room to ear-splittingly loud jazz or the Sex Pistols. He was also doing voluntary work at a stable, supporting people who were seriously ill so that they could enjoy riding, and he'd made lots more friends through that.

One night he phoned me in France and said that he had had a letter from the hospital where he had been treated for his heart attack. They had reviewed his records and X-rays and wanted him to come in for a chat. They had made him an appointment. The letter was from the Oncology Department.

I went back to the UK and, with my sister, accompanied Dad to his appointment at King's College Hospital in London.

It wasn't good news. Doctors checking the X-rays had noticed a shadow in his chest.

'Give it to me straight, Doc,' said my dad as my sister and I held hands tightly under the desk, hoping and hoping that they wouldn't say the worst. It was déjà vu: the memories of discovering Mum was ill were still horribly raw.

'It's lung cancer. You have two years, maybe, if you respond to treatment. It is inoperable,' said the doctor gently, placing a hand on Dad's shoulder. It's a rotten job sometimes.

My dad was a fighter all his life. Both he and my mum had awful childhoods in inner London. Poor, often hungry, not well cared for and rather broken young people, they had found each other in their teens and been together from the day they met at my mum's engagement party to her then boyfriend. Dad was a rascal and was at the party with a friend of a friend. He'd never met my mum before but he swept her off her feet when he wrote her name in ink on his dazzling white shirt sleeve and begged her to meet him and go to the cinema. My mum broke off her engagement and within months they married, and most of the time adored each other.

My dad had counted every single day since she died and every time I spoke to him he would tell me the exact number: 'Your mother died two years, three months and twelve days ago today . . . Your mother died four years, eight months and eight days ago today . . . Your mother died six years, nine months and seventeen days ago today.' Every night, he kissed a photo of her before going to bed.

When we left the hospital, my dad told us to pull ourselves together after we broke down.

'Your mother died seven years, eight months and nineteen days ago today,' he said, his voice cracking, and it was hard not to sob out loud on the train going back to his house. He hated a fuss.

'I feel fine and I want to carry on living a normal life but I might need some help,' he said.

It was almost as if being told that he had cancer induced the physical symptoms, which we hadn't yet seen any signs of. My sister, who lived close by, took on the majority of the daily tasks like shopping and cooking. I travelled back and forth between France and England and went with him to his appointments and to his chemotherapy sessions. I'd stay for a few days to cook and be there when he needed company, someone to talk to and to make him feel cared for. When he was feeling better he came out to France and we enjoyed going to restaurants, bars, supermarkets, markets — everywhere he went he would charm and flirt outrageously with the ladies. Even though he had never quite forgiven me for giving up the chance to be a director in a bank, he came to love my village and this part of France. I like to think that he knew that I would be happy here.

Dad remained fiercely independent, although it was mostly us who drove him to and from France, as he was an awful driver at the best of times. Once, he decided to come out on the ferry alone. Often I travel as a foot passenger on P&O Ferries — it's so easy. For most people, at least. It is a ninety-minute journey across the Channel and takes no more than twenty minutes or so to disembark and get through customs. We were to meet him at 3 p.m. He was still very spritely at that stage, despite his illness, and he couldn't abide people mentioning it; he wanted to act normal, as he put it, for as long as possible.

His ferry arrived in the port. The foot passengers came through customs where we were waiting but there was no sign of Dad. He didn't answer his mobile phone. I went to the information desk and asked if it was possible to see if they had my dad's name on the passenger list, as he hadn't disembarked with the other passengers. Perhaps he had missed the boat. They checked. His name was there. By now I was getting really stressed, convinced something awful had happened, that he'd collapsed on the ferry, perhaps, and was lying under a table unseen. The woman at the information desk called the purser on board to ask for information. We were asked to sit in a waiting area while they searched for the missing passenger. All sorts of horrible scenarios ran through my head.

Fifteen minutes later I heard my dad's voice: 'There she is. There's my daughter.' He was laughing loudly as he came through the passenger control area, flanked on either side by two men in uniform.

'Is this yours?' asked one of them, and I think I saw an element of sympathy in his face, but it might just have been extreme irritation.

'Erm, yes, that's my dad.'

'We found him in the bar,' said the security man. 'He hadn't heard the announcement that we had landed and he should disembark . . . on account of the fact that he has had several glasses of whisky, it seems.'

'I had one glass,' hiccupped Dad.

'He's all yours,' said the man. That was the last time we let Dad come out on the ferry on his own.

Work slowed on the house while I spent half my time in France and half in the UK, living with Dad, sleeping on a blow-up bed in the spare room. Some days were good, some were bad, and some were very bad.

I adored Dad and grew closer than ever to him. I was grateful to have the chance to make sure he knew how important he was to me before it was too late. He was quite a gruff character, hated sentimentality and found it hard to open up to anyone. I only ever saw him cry twice: when my mum died and when we visited the American Cemetery in Normandy.

We worked our way through some of the things he had on his bucket list, which mostly revolved around food and cars. We went motor racing at Brands Hatch, enjoyed afternoon tea at Harrods and dinner at Simpson's in the Strand. We sat at a table at the back of the room surveying its legendary grandeur and drank champagne while Dad told me how, as a little boy, he lived not far away and would sit outside, cold and hungry, 'watching all the posh people, all these nobs in their finery' going into this historic restaurant. He had always wanted to eat there and when he did it was a bittersweet moment as we realized that many of the other things on his bucket list would never be fulfilled.

When brain cancer was diagnosed, Dad was told he couldn't drive any more. His beloved Jaguar had to be sold and he made friends with all the local taxi drivers, who would ferry him around, taking him to the shops, bridge club (he was by then a grand master), the doctors, the dog racing track, the betting shop. Gambling was always one of his great loves: even on my wedding day he was in the betting shop and almost missed the ceremony, making my mum as angry as hell. All the wedding photos show her with a pinched face and Dad with an 'oops, I've done it again' smile.

His friends and family rallied round and it was a mixed time of joy and pure misery. When he came out to France he would get his 'fix' by driving the ride-on lawn mower, frequently crashing it into fences. Once he drove into a stone birdbath that my mum had given me. He broke it in half and almost upended himself and we had to ban him from driving the lawn mower as well, in case he got hurt.

I spent many days just sitting quietly in a chair in my dad's house, not making a sound as he slept fitfully on the sofa. He refused to go to bed during the daytime even though he was exhausted, reeling from the results of chemo and the pills he was taking on a trial programme. The doctors had explained the trial wouldn't help him, it might even have some nasty side effects, but what they would learn from his experience would benefit cancer patients in the future. He signed up immediately.

I passed the time at Dad's house by writing about my life in France, the things I saw and the places I went.

When Dad woke up he'd ask me what I'd been doing and I'd read him my scribblings.

'You should write something,' he said one day. 'Your mother was a great writer but she never had the confidence to see it through and write a whole book.'

The inevitable, unwanted time came when my dad had to go into the same hospice that my mum had been in. When the administrative staff told me the room number Dad was to have, I was shocked: it was the same room Mum had died in. I wanted them to try to change it but he said he was happy to be in that room where his beloved had been nine years, nine months and twelve days before. Where he had sat and held her hand tenderly and told her gently that it was okay to go, that it was time to sleep, to rest. I had sat beside him, weeping quietly, hardly daring to breathe as I witnessed true love, and watched him let her go.

Two days after going into the hospice, Dad passed away. It was a little over two years since he was diagnosed, almost exactly as the doctor had predicted.

He was a reprobate, difficult, generous, intelligent, brave and sometimes badly behaved, and he taught me that life is something that must be treasured and that every minute counts. I went back to France determined to make a success of my new life.

14

' I say potatoes you say pommes de terre

I am British — we queue. In fact, we are a nation that is, on the whole, extremely good at standing in a line in front of an entrance, cash desk or anywhere else, waiting for our turn. We may even take a sandwich and a flask of tea with us if we think it might be a prolonged affair. If anyone should presume to sneak in front of us, we will cast a sly look around to see if someone else has noticed and roll our eyes at each other. We will heave a deeply disappointed and disapproving sigh. Someone will say, 'Excuse me, there's a queue here,' and everyone will stare at the lawbreaker. Usually, the queue jumper/criminal will shuffle off pretending he or she hadn't noticed the long line of patient lemmings.

What happens in France goes against all my British instincts. French people push in.

In a shop, at a bus stop, in the bank, at the cinema, in a café, ticket office or anywhere else you have to queue.

They use bags and umbrellas, elbows and

knees. They use their bodies as battering rams. Elderly French people who look so frail you might think they could hardly lift a feather seem to find renewed energy when faced with a queue. Their skin brightens, they limber up on the edge of the line, they straighten their backs and smooth their wispy hair and, va va voom, they dash to the front, knocking out the opposition with walking sticks and Zimmer frames, or with trolleys if you're in a supermarket, one of the favourite hunting grounds for queue jumpers in France.

One summer at a village event in which two hundred of us attended a lunch in a tent, the spit-roasted pig cooking in the canvas kitchen caught fire in rather spectacular fashion. We were not evacuated from the tent while the *pompiers* (firefighters) rushed to the rescue and doused the flaming cochon. Oh no, none of that health and safety nonsense. Instead the kitchen staff made rum punch and handed it out liberally to keep us quiet and in our seats (they didn't want to do refunds) until they could return to continue the cooking.

A lethal mix of dark and white rum and a piddling amount of orange juice, combined with the heat of the summer sun and a blazing kitchen — there was only ever going to be one outcome.

When it was announced with great fanfare that lunch was at last being served and we should form an orderly queue, it was like a stampede at the Pamplona bull run. Grown men and women fought with each other to get to the front. My neighbour Jean-Claude and his wife were on our table. He jumped to his feet and dragged Mark with him, dead-legging anyone who got in the way, pushing Mark in front of him to use as a human shield.

The servers plopped charred meat and hunks of bread unceremoniously on plates as fast as they could to move the arguing, swearing, fighting queue on, and eventually order was restored and everyone acted as if nothing had happened.

This attitude towards waiting in line spills on to the roads of France. A line of traffic will cause an immediate angry reaction from a French driver.

Driving in my part of France is generally a pleasure after London; you usually only witness gridlock when cows are crossing the road. But as soon as a French person spots a car going more slowly than he thinks it should, he seems to consider it his absolute duty to overtake, no matter the circumstances. The change from normal, happily driving French person to road-raging fiend, be it a ninety-year-old man who can hardly see or a usually calm and sweet-natured woman, happens in an instant — they all seem to turn into maniacs behind the wheel.

Although I drive at the regulatory speed, I've been overtaken on hairpin bends, with a heavy goods vehicle convoy in front of me, on blind corners, on roads with signs saying no overtaking and in the dark in thick snow. The hand gestures used in the UK when communicating in such circumstances appear to be just as well understood in France.

I don't know if it's because they are genuinely all in a rush or if they just don't like being behind a foreign car, but I have a feeling that any sign of authority turns some French people from really nice, friendly, cultured people into wannabe anarchists.

In the rural town of Desvres not far from where we live, there's an old church in the town centre with a big sign saying '*Defense d'uriner*'. Now you, like me, might think that it was unnecessary to put up a sign forbidding people to urinate on the wall of a church. What that sign appears to have achieved is actually to encourage it. Twice I've witnessed a man relieving himself directly under the notice.

French people also take umbrage when the

road rules are updated. Take *priorite á droite*, for instance — a strange and frankly dangerous rule that gives drivers priority to enter a road from the right without stopping, including on main roads. This isn't on all routes — only where the *priorité à droite* sign is displayed, which actually makes it even more treacherous, because it's completely random. It appears to be a case of national pride and a test of will where any French driver may utilize this crazy law without stopping or looking. It is the cause of many accidents and the government has been attempting to phase it out. You wouldn't know that where I live: there are still dozens of roads allowing this practice. Even when the road sign is amended to a 'give way' sign and lines are painted on the road to indicate to the driver entering from a right-hand road that priority is no longer theirs, locals invariably ignore it because they don't think the rule should be changed.

In the Café du Centre in Fruges, which looks as if it hasn't altered in sixty years, Mark and I sat sipping coffee that could wake a hibernating polar bear in the middle of winter, discussing with Madame the proprietor whether the French have anarchistic tendencies.

'Not at all,' she said, turning to greet a

customer who had just parked his VSP outside the café.

What, you may ask, is a VSP? It stands for *voiture sans permis* — a car you can drive without a licence. Incredibly to anyone not born in France, it is permitted to drive a particular type of car without taking or passing a driving test. From the age of fourteen, youths may drive these cars after spending seven hours in one with someone who is qualified to drive. This means that if someone loses their licence for drink-related offences or dangerous driving, they may still drive, albeit in a car that doesn't go very fast, as the speed is limited to 45 km/h, although manufacturers are working on models that may go faster.

'Aurellian,' said Madame to the VSP driver, 'do you think we French are anarchistic in nature?'

'Yes, of course,' he said. 'But we are also not anarchistic. Take me. I cannot, as we all know, drive my van because I just happened to have a little sip too much one time and I got caught. So they take away my licence. I comply with the rules, as I am not an anarchist. But I drive my little clown car out there which I am allowed to do and I wave to that gendarme who stopped me and made me lose my licence and I thumb my nose at him, and that, I think, is anarchistic.'

Aurellian sipped his red wine, looking quietly pleased with himself and then disappointed with us for not carrying on the conversation. We know better. French people absolutely love to debate. If there is a way to say something using a hundred words instead of ten, you can be absolutely sure they will go for it. Every single event I have ever been to in France has started late because, given an opportunity to make a speech, a French person simply cannot pass up the chance. A French audience accepts this as normal; foreigners are completely bemused by it. Whether it is the opening of a road, a restaurant or a concert, everything that can possibly be started with a long drawn-out dialogue is considered an opportunity to use the skills of language, a highly prized talent — there is no such thing as someone who talks too much in France. Sometimes debates sound like arguments — full-on, abusive, yelling-at-each-other rows. Monsieur and Madame Jupe, who live across the road, often scream at each other, trading insults and accusations that anyone who walks by, or lives opposite them like me, can hear. Jean-Claude tells me that this is seen as a sign of a healthy relationship: your partnership is close enough that you can talk to each other this way and still be friends, lovers, or married even, after it's over. He has a point, perhaps.

While Mark and I contemplated the complete weirdness of being able to drive a car when one is banned from driving a car, we could hear strange noises, like someone strangling a cat. Four skinny men dressed in tight leather trousers and jackets, and sporting bandanas and sunglasses, appeared through the back door of the café, tuning up their instruments — two trumpets, a drum and a harmonica. They gave a quick rendition of 'Desmond has a barrow in the market place — Ob-la-di ob-la-dah' in strong French accents and then wandered out. It's that sort of town: friendly and ever so slightly odd.

Fruges is not a showy place, but there are some interesting buildings and a public water tap where the locals help themselves to free mineral water, and the people there are welcoming. So, when I saw that Mathilde Paris, an architect in the town and also the proprietor of the Bulot Gourmand restaurant, was organizing a party to celebrate the restaurant's first very successful year, my friend Kat and I jumped at the opportunity to have a girls' night out. Kat is an Australian from the outback, a textile designer who came to France to house-sit in our village. Seduced by the gorgeous countryside of the

Seven Valleys and the affordable house prices, she and her Greek husband couldn't bear to leave when their house-sit was up, and so they bought a house the other side of the valley where they grow wonderful vegetables in their hilltop garden. Kat uses the vegetables as inspiration for the beautiful linen she makes at her quirky farmhouse. The party was held at the Domaine de la Traxène, the local 'castle farm', which I'd passed umpteen times and had been itching to get inside and have a look at, having watched it progress from a total wreck to a restored beauty.

The party was due to start at 8 p.m. and we arrived on time. It was a Mexican-themed night and there was a band and dancers; the proprietor (dressed as a cactus) and her band of helpers were handing out big strong glasses of punch. The French tend to eat dinner much later than foreigners so we sat for the first course around 10 p.m. — by then we were pretty happy!

French people really know how to let their hair down. I don't know if it's because on the whole very little happens in the countryside so when it does they make the most of it, or if they just really like to party. Put on a funky tune and it seems you can't keep a French person down — there was Mexican dancing, line dancing, disco dancing, ballroom dancing and cha-chas.

There was singing too, and I was utterly amazed that so many people knew the words to Irish folk songs, which it seems are very popular in this area.

I have no idea what time the dancing stopped, as Kat and I, lightweights, left in the early hours of the morning while they were still going strong, boogying to 'Mambo No. 5'. The air is pure here, and the sky was filled with stars looking bigger and brighter than I had ever seen before. A full moon lit the way home; there are no lamp posts on these quiet country lanes, which were deserted apart from a hare, an owl and a hawk, startled from their places by the car's headlamps. What they made of the noise from the party that echoed round the valley we can only guess.

I had another chance to test the theory that French people are party animals soon after this when friends invited Mark and me to a beer festival near Hesdin in the local *salle des fêtes*.

Adverts for the Soiree Bavaroise were plastered on posts in towns for miles around: '*Venez nombreux*,' they urged, come in numbers, the fun will start at 7 p.m. We'd arranged to meet a dozen friends there. The British contingent, of course, arrived on time, though I am not sure why, as we all know by now that nothing ever starts when it is supposed to. Our French friends sensibly arrived closer to 9 p.m., as did almost everyone else, with some people still arriving when we left after midnight.

The menu was *choucroute* (sauerkraut) and sausages. Despite my apprehension that we'd have to queue for it, creating a French-style storming of the buffet table complete with punch-ups, in fact the food was served à table — the starters arrived at 9.45 p.m. by which time many of the British men had had several glasses of beer.

Since the north of France is famous for beer, I expected there to be lots of choice, but no, there were just two beers to choose from and a much longer wine list that also included champagne — a very French German beer festival.

The 'Austrian oompah band' was in fact French and played mostly French music including 'Le Madison' several times. In my part of France it's a very popular tune, and has been since the 1960s. French people are loyal to the point of obsessiveness sometimes. A case in point is Johnny Hallyday, who is the French equivalent of Elvis. Johnny continues to fill huge stadiums for his concerts and you can't go anywhere in France without seeing at least one person wearing a T-shirt with his image on.

'Le Madison' is obligatory at any and every sort of French celebration where I live. It's a catchy song, sounding a bit like the old *Batman* TV series theme tune, and as soon as people hear the first few bars, they all rush to the dance floor, form up in lines and start their moves.

It looked like a really easy dance, so I dragged one of my friends up to the dance floor to join in. As soon as my back was turned she sat down and left me there on my own, right at the front of the heaving rows of line dancers. To my surprise and dismay I discovered it's not that easy at all. I missed all the little jumps, and was facing left when everyone else went right. But, at events such as this, making an idiot of yourself is obligatory so no one took any notice whatsoever of the left-footed English woman.

Generally speaking, the place to socialize is the café-bar in Hucqueliers, a short drive away. It is a hotbed of gossip, rumours and intellectual debate. Discussions about the goings-on at the Elysée Palace are conducted as if we are all on first-name terms with the president and his nearest and dearest. If you didn't know better, you'd think old Monsieur Dubarre — who we all know has never been further than Picardy — spent the week in Paris as an invisible spy 'comme cul et chemise' with government officials, says his daughter Annie behind his back. It translates literally as to get along like one's buttocks and shirt, and means 'as thick as thieves'.

The bar is open pretty much when the proprietor feels like opening it, which is some lunchtimes but not all and some evenings, and never on a Sunday or national holiday. It closes early because he likes to watch TV and, as he says, 'there is more to life than all métro-boulot-dodo', the French expression that implies that your day is all hard grind (literally metro-work-sleep).

The escapades of those in power in France are the subject of much debate in the bar. Although generally the French are happy for certain things not to be reported in newspapers, claiming that even the president deserves privacy, they nevertheless seem to enjoy talking about it just as much as the rest of us.

They have been scandalized in recent years by some of the behaviour of public figures, the mudslinging between a president's exes, for instance, and a one-time potential candidate's shenanigans with prostitutes in a hotel in Lille.

'I can't really understand what all the fuss

is about — it's hardly in Italian Prime Minister's Berlusconi's Bunga Bunga league after all,' I said, but apparently the French washing of dirty linen in public is simply not acceptable. On the whole, to my amazement, my French friends prefer that the media keep the lid on things. There are times when they may be right. I do recall reading that Cheri Blair once said that Tony still excited her in all ways, which left me quite traumatized and wishing a lid had been firmly kept on that little nugget.

The bar is also the place to go when you want to know what is going on in the village or anywhere in France, it seems. And if I want to visit somewhere I haven't been before, this is where I can get the insider's view.

One evening I mentioned that I had visited the mill of Lugy not far from Fruges. The family who own it mill organic flour, make bread and teach bread-making the old way with their massive old wood oven known as 'la grand-mère'. On the way, I had passed through the next village of Verchin, where I saw a magnificent church in the Gothic style, with ornate patterns on its façade and lovely tall arched stained glass windows. But it was the twisted spire that made this place really stick in my memory; in most countries it would be a landmark, a tourist site of great repute, but here it's just another old church.

'Did you notice the slits in the walls?' asked one of the bar regulars. 'That's where the archers used to fire arrows on the English invaders.' Everyone fell about laughing. They take great joy in reminding me that I am one of their ancient enemies. It's no good me pointing out that my paternal heritage is in fact Italian. As far as they are concerned, I am a rosbif.

'That spire, though,' I went on, trying to get off the subject of our historic enmity (even if it was 600 years ago). 'It's incredible how warped it is.'

Twisted spires are caused by the wood structure drying out, but Monsieur Dubarre was totally dismissive of such a dull reason.

'Bah oui, but you know the young girls of the village in days gone by had poor manners and loose morals, and when a virgin arrived at the doors of the church for her wedding the church spire was so astonished that it leaned over to look and when it arose, it was twisted!' He stopped and looked around to make sure we had appreciated the story.

'The spire will only unwind if such a strange thing occurs a second time!' he added, and then he winked and roared with laughter. His daughter says he has been telling this tale for decades and when he is gone she will tell the tale and teach her son to tell it too so that the legend is not lost.

It doesn't matter where I go, how far away it is or how obscure, someone in the bar will know of it, will have been there and will have a story to tell.

I visited Marseille: 'Bah, they are all crooks.' I visited Lyon: 'Bah, they think they are all chefs.' I visited Paris: 'Bah, they are all rude.'

If you live in a village in France and you want to know what the mayor is thinking of doing, although I'm not sure why you would, just go to the local bar. Someone will have the sort of knowledge that politicians would pay highly to keep quiet and newspaper editors would sell their grandmothers to get. Did I know that the mayor of such and such village has been siphoning off the common land secretly, putting a fence around it, hoping that the villagers will forget its existence? Had I heard that the English lady councillor in a village close by has been causing all manner of problems because she opposes everything the mayor says for the 'fun of it'?

What will the weather be like in a week's time? Go to my local bar, the one in Hucqueliers, where Monsieur Legrand will reveal all. He studies ants, newts, moles and frogs and is, I have to admit, generally far more accurate than the weather report. And the customers are full of helpful advice, although I'm never quite sure how much of it is real or made up. One man told me that when it gets very cold, you have to be careful to check that the feet of your chickens or ducks have not got stuck in the frozen ground. I have never seen it for myself but he assured me that he has had to chisel several ducks out over the years.

There is all manner of gossip to be found out in the bar, the source of much of it being the pharmacy, I am sure, where your most intimate conversations may be overheard. French people seem to be obsessed with ailments and medicine. There is typically a queue at the pharmacy and people leave weighed down with enormous bags full of pills and potions. There is always a chair in the shop for those who don't have the stamina to stand in line for hours, as the pharmacy is the one place where people seem content to wait their turn, calmly chatting away about this and that. The chair is always occupied by a little old lady who looks as though butter wouldn't melt in her mouth. But, beware, she is listening to everything that is said and will certainly share the news with her cronies.

15

Flop chef, not top chef

We had heard a lot about how good the French health service is, but had been lucky enough not to have had cause to try it. This all changed when Mark was struck with a mysterious illness that made him very sick. Like many men, he is averse to going to the doctors but, after a week of him eating dry toast and moaning, I'd had enough.

Me: 'Right, that's it, I am going to make you an appointment with the English-speaking doctor in town.'

Mark: 'I'll be better by the time we get an appointment.'

We were both used to London waiting times where, as a general rule, you need to make an appointment days, if not weeks, in advance. I phoned anyway. It was 9 a.m.

'Can you come in at 11.30 a.m.?' asked the doctor, who answered his own phone.

My jaw hit the floor in shock.

The doctor's office is a room in a converted old mansion house. It has seen better days, but who's complaining when you only sit for five minutes in the waiting room and then go straight in?

'I love English patients,' said the doctor. 'You don't mind waiting a few hours for an appointment. My French patients start screaming if it's longer than thirty minutes!'

That day he organized for Mark to have blood and various other tests, the results of which came back two days later. We phoned the doctor for an update and, although the cause wasn't clear, it was nothing serious. Later we discovered Mark had developed an allergy to certain thickening products in processed food, which he had been eating a lot of when I was in London with Dad.

It was a wake-up call.

It is a well-known fact among my friends that I am useless in the kitchen. I have no interest in cooking. When I worked in London I lived on takeaways of all sorts, not just because it was usually too late to make anything except for toast but because I didn't want to cook. Mark says that the issue is not that I can't cook but that I'd rather be doing something else. It's true. I start cooking, go and look at my Facebook page, or read emails and that is far more interesting so I sit a little longer and forget completely what I am supposed to be doing in the kitchen. Most people use a timer to alert them to when their dishes are ready to serve; for me it's often the smell of burning.

Of course, we all know about French cooking and the national love of good food and wine that is not just a hobby, but practically mandatory. However, I was totally unprepared for the shock-horror reaction of my French friends when it came to the subject of gastronomy and me. In the same way that we Brits are obsessed with talking about the weather, the French are fanatical about food.

In my village, everyone, and I mean everyone, grows vegetables and fruit in their gardens; many of them additionally rent or borrow a bit of field and some of them are farmers. Nearly everyone keeps chickens and often ducks, geese, quail and various other birds too. For a short while Jean-Claude had a peacock that he found in the road behind the local church.

Jean-Claude's peacock was the talk of the town until the owner, a South African expat from 5 kilometres away, got to hear about it through the grapevine and reclaimed it. Everyone in the village heaved a sigh of relief, as it was horribly noisy and screeched day and night.

Food is a common denominator here so, when we first came to the region, whenever I met someone new in the village, they always wanted to share their tips with me — the best market for fish (Etaples), for vegetables (Saint-Omer), the best butcher, the best baker, cake maker, cheese shop, wine store, restaurant, bar, café, pork farm, beef farm, chicken farm . . . the list was endless. Of course, I thanked them and took notes. It only became a problem when they asked me things like, 'Did you see the fabulous asparagus at the market at Montreuil-sur-Mer this morning — we're making *asparagus à la roi*, what will you do with yours?', or 'Monsieur T has made some marvellous rillettes this week, I can tell you where he buys his ingredients,' with a wink.

In the end I had to confess: I can't cook. When I first told my neighbour Claudette of my lack of culinary skills she was horrified and cast an eye of sympathy to Mark. He is hardly wasting away, so her concern is really not needed.

'At your age? You can't cook?'

It was clear that my admission made me seem, as far as the French were concerned, a complete and utter failure. It was also taken as a challenge.

Claudette was eighty-four years old at that time, fiercely independent and very determined. She cooks a three-course lunch every day, and though Bernadette, her only child, isn't able to indulge as she works in an office and likes to go out with her friends, Jean-Claude, her son-in-law, drives past our house each day, regular as clockwork on the dot of noon, to join her for lunch. Soup, a hot meal and a dessert.

Claudette prepares everything from scratch; she told me she has never been in a supermarket in her life and has no intention of doing so. She does, though, confess that Bernadette buys her shampoo sometimes — she no longer makes it herself as she used to.

In the entrance to Claudette's farmhouse is a cloth to wipe your feet before you take your place at a table in the kitchen; there's no hallway, so you go straight into this main room. Almost all the old farmhouses in this village have a table in the first room you enter from the front door. This is where you'll be invited to sit and chat, are offered a glass of something or a cup of coffee or hot chocolate. Claudette wears a house coat every day, a sort of sleeveless pinafore dress that does up with buttons at the front and keeps the clothes underneath clean. Everyone seems to have them here and I have instructed Mark to take me to a psychiatrist if I ever show any signs of wanting to wear one. Claudette is a wonderfully fit old lady whose energy seems to know no bounds and I had to know how she does it, so one day, when I found myself seated with a glass of red wine in her kitchen, I asked her what the secret is.

'Here on this oven, every morning, I cook myself a slice of pork for breakfast,' said Claudette.

She told me she has used the same oven for more than sixty years. It was a wedding present and not a day has gone by when it has not been in use. It is a beauty, shaped like the front of a row boat, a bright blue beast, covered with enamelled flowers of all colours. It looks like it wouldn't be out of place in an old-fashioned fairground. Fuelled by coal and wood, it is the bane of her family's life, since they have to cut the wood into small pieces for it all year round. It is not just for cooking but heats the water, too, so it is permanently on whatever the weather.

'Then I pour myself a glass of cider, home-made is best. That is what gives me my strength and keeps me going.'

Home-made cider is very popular in these parts. Wild apple trees are everywhere, and in the autumn months a waft of warm, fermenting apple will often drift out from barns or garages in all the little villages in this valley.

'Life doesn't need to be too complicated

and I keep mine simple, which also keeps me young,' she added, and then told me that she had never been on an aeroplane. In fact, she has never been further than 30 kilometres from the village.

'Don't you wish you had seen more of the world?' I asked. I love to travel, I told her, and I go all over France by train. 'Don't you regret that you have never been to Paris or Rome, to London or Venice? Don't you want to go somewhere exotic or even urban? Don't you wonder what it would be like to go on an aeroplane?'

'No,' she said with feeling. 'Everyone I love, everything I need, it is here, in this village. My family, my friends, all that I hold dear.'

Then she added, 'Well, perhaps one thing I would have liked . . . to see the Queen.' She adores the British Royal Family. When Prince William married Kate Middleton, Claudette was glued to her black and white TV set in her cosy kitchen. I say cosy — I mean hellishly hot.

Pride of place on the oven goes to a William and Kate tea towel. It is certainly strange that since the French cut off the heads of their own royal family they have taken the British lot to heart.

Claudette decided my lack of kitchen skills was not acceptable and she set to work attempting to teach me the basics of rustic recipes.

And it wasn't only her. Before long, word got out (there are no secrets in a French village) that the English woman was not only an ex-townie, she was also an idiot in the kitchen and needed help.

We have our bread delivered to our homes here in the middle of nowhere by a man in a van. The shops are miles away and for many old people the mobile stores are a lifeline, and for everyone else a real time saver, not to mention ecologically friendly. I leave a bag hanging over the gate and the bread man pops a loaf in as he goes by three times a week. One day he knocked on the door.

'Bonjour, Monsieur bread man.'

'Bonjour, useless cook.'

'Pardon?'

Well, no, he didn't actually call me that, but he might as well have done. It had come to his attention — someone in the next village had mentioned it — that Madame Merde could not cook.

'It is easy to cook. Everyone can cook.'

'I don't really want to cook.'

'But you must cook. It is the law.'

No, he didn't say that either, but again, he might as well have done.

He handed me a piece of paper with some writing on.

'Here is how to make bread.'

Bread? Me make bread? He was the bloody bread man, what was he thinking? I thanked him and off he went on his merry way.

After that, every week he would pop a recipe in the post box: how to make vanilla ice cream, beef casserole, buttery biscuits, simple cakes (nobody thought I would ever be able to tackle anything complicated) — a random array of goodies. This went on for months until one day the baker who made the bread had a heart attack and the deliveries stopped while he recovered, after which the bread man got another job and I never saw him again. We have a new bread man now and he does not leave me recipes.

Meanwhile, Claudette had realized that I was never going to be a star pupil and had resorted to coaching me in the basics, like her version of French toast. Eventually I gave up trying not to cook and managed to make her a passable onion soup, which got me off the hook and allowed Claudette to stop her lessons.

Actually, I never did learn to make that soup. It turned out that Mark, who had never cooked before in his life, had a feel for food, as it were. He got it. He understood the chemistry of mixing ingredients together, he appreciated the value of flavours and he rolled up his sleeves and started cooking. When Claudette sent me home with her passed-down-through-the-generations recipe for French onion soup I merely passed it to Mark to make.

'Claudette says that onions are an aphrodisiac,' I told him in an effort to drum up some enthusiasm. 'I reckon it's worth a go.' She told me that in the old days, when country folk wed, the morning after they would be served a bowl of steaming hot onion soup to replenish flagging energy. I can't honestly say that the soup had any effect on us, but when I took a bowl to Claudette to assess my efforts, she announced it was 'quite good' and that was the last time she tried to teach me.

Mark, however, went from strength to strength in the kitchen, turning out cakes and pastry, stews and stir-fries. His grandmother had been a pastry cook in her youth, working for a rich family in a grand house. When Mark was a little boy and she was long retired but made cakes the family still talk about, he would watch her bake in her tiny kitchen and be allowed to lick the spoon. Whether it was the memory of that or just that he likes to win, cooking seems to be in his veins.

We are both agreed: in this house he is top

chef and I am flop chef.

Although I don't like cooking food that much, I sure like to eat it, and I don't think there's anywhere more interesting than France when it comes to great dishes. They're not always perfect, however.

Crow pâté doesn't really do it for me but Jean-Claude swears by it and makes it often. I'm not that keen on snails either, though I have tried them. I consider myself quite adventurous when it comes to food — I'll almost always order something on the menu if I don't have a clue what it is, just for the fun of it. This can be good and bad. Once in the lovely covered market in Dijon I had snail cake.

This market is gastronomically gorgeous. Designed by a son of Dijon, Gustave Eiffel of Eiffel Tower fame, the building's blue metal framework is really quite beautiful and the stalls that are laid out below its high roof are full of delectable delicacies. The producers, artisans and sellers are incredibly proud of their wares and when I was offered a taste tour it was a great honour. Gingerbread dipped in chocolate — yum; local cheese — delicious. All manner of goodies were displayed, but the best was being saved for last, I was told. I heard the word gâteau, which I knew meant cake, but the plate that

165

was offered to me held a chunk of something grey and slimy looking.

'Gâteau what did you say?' I asked.

'Gâteau *moelleux aux escargots de Bourgogne*, soft snail cake, a local speciality.'

Ah yes, that will be what that slippery-looking head is hanging out the end there, I thought to myself, not with much relish. But you have to try these things, so I popped the chunk in my mouth and chewed . . . and chewed. You've heard that expression that something is an acquired taste; well, I haven't acquired a taste for snail cake and I'm not sure I ever will or even want to.

Many people tend to think that French cuisine cannot possibly be bad. Ever. It can. I promise you it can.

One bitterly cold winter weekend, our friends Karen and Joe were staying with us and we decided to go out to lunch. We had by now become accustomed to phoning to reserve a table before venturing out, as it seems quite normal in the countryside for restaurants to close with no rhyme or reason. Even phoning to check doesn't work sometimes. I took my dad to the D-Day commemorations in Normandy one year and we decided to go to a restaurant that had a good reputation according to the lady in the boulangerie. She was right — we went there for lunch, it was very friendly and they served good, rustic, tasty food.

'What nights are you open, as we'd like to come back?'

'We're open every night ... except Tuesday, Wednesday and Sunday.'

'Okay, can we book a table for Thursday at eight p.m.?'

'Yes.'

We went back on Thursday night. It was shut.

As the lunch with Karen and Joe was a spur of the moment decision we hadn't actually booked anywhere. We warned them it wasn't easy to find somewhere open in the country. We thought that if we went to a town, we'd have more choice. We ended up in Berck-sur-Mer, a lovely seaside resort about thirty minutes away, famous for its bracing air. As it was the week between Christmas and New Year, almost everything was shut. Only one small restaurant was open. In hindsight, it did look a bit dubious from the outside and normally we would never have gone in. We've been to Berck-sur-Mer many times since and found some fabulous restaurants.

We were met by the sight of ten or so unloved rickety wooden tables that were certainly not prepared for diners. Not that there were any. A wooden bar ran the length of one wall, local and Belgian beer pumps lined the edge of it, bottles of apéritifs sat higgledy piggledy on shelves. It was rather dark and completely silent and I knew immediately that we should simply back out right now. Karen, meanwhile, was enchanted with the 'Frenchness' of it. As she came from Hammersmith in west London, I could see that she might find this place quaint, with its old tiled floor, old tired furniture and the old mad barman who now lunged into view from the swing door at the back.

'Bonjour,' he yelled loudly. 'Sit, sit. Do you want an apéritif?'

With this he lurched to the bar and poured himself a glass of absinthe, an action that was clearly not a novelty to him on this cold miserable day.

It was mesmerizing to watch him. He had an enormous nose. It was very red and speckled, like a freshly plucked chicken, and so big that, when he lifted the glass to his lips, he had to tip his head back and flick his long black quiff away from his eyes and then tip the liquid into his mouth, as it did not fit in the glass.

'I didn't even know you could get absinthe,' whispered Karen. 'I thought it was banned because it made you go mad.'

She wasn't entirely wrong. It was banned for many years after a tragic incident in the early 1900s in which a Swiss man killed his wife and children and then tried to kill himself after drinking absinthe. He had drunk it for three days without stopping to sleep, though. It wasn't until the 1980s that it was quietly reintroduced in France. This time with half the alcoholic strength but with its reputation for inducing mania intact.

We considered trying a drop of absinthe ourselves. In fact, I thought that a touch of self-induced madness might get us through the terror of eating there, but everyone else decided we'd had quite enough fun for one day, having been caught up in a village scandal.

Mid-morning, Jean-Claude had knocked on the door, red-faced and puffing with the effort of rushing up the hill. This alone would have been enough to alert the local media, as it was highly unusual for him not to drive his van the short distance. He didn't wait for me to say bonjour or exchange kisses.

'Come quick, there are burglars in the chemin,' he wheezed before rushing back out of the gate. 'Hurry, you must come — and get Mark.'

I wasn't sure that I'd heard right, but he seemed pretty shaken up so the four of us donned coats and boots and wandered down the road to the *chemin*, a little alleyway that runs to one side of our hilly road. There are just a couple of houses in the chemin, both of which were holiday homes at that time and empty most of the year. Jean-Claude was hopping up and down outside the end house and when he saw us he came rushing over.

'There's someone in the house that shouldn't be there,' he whispered with a great deal of theatrical flair. 'I've called the mayor and the gendarmes but we must keep watch.'

He then positioned Mark and Joe outside the house where the burglars were, and told Karen and me to remain at the end of the alley where it meets our little road in case the intruders tried to escape. He himself would go down to the main road and wait for the gendarmes so that he could direct them to the scene of the crime.

We stood there for ten minutes, chatting about whether the burglars might be violent if they came out. We weren't worried as we were certain Mark and Joe could handle any situation, as they both liked to box and do martial arts. Eventually, we heard sirens in the distance and to our astonishment two vans containing nine police officers and a sniffer dog screeched to a halt.

Looking splendid in their uniforms and

drawing their guns, they proceeded with cautious determination to the empty house.

'Stand back,' said their leader. 'This could be very dangerous.'

At that, a female police officer herded the four of us down the *chemin*, the alley, and into the road where Jean-Claude was giving a statement.

'I was walking along to my barn, which is in the *chemin*, when I saw the window of the house of the owners-who-never-come-out was broken. There was movement. I ran to call the police. That's it.'

'Did you see anyone, Monsieur?'

'Yes.'

'Who?'

'I don't know. There were two of them, though. Men.'

The burglars were, of course, long gone, but the police team carried out forensic checks. They dusted the windows and surfaces in the house for fingerprints, took photos, looked for clues and made copious notes before departing, watched by all the kids in the village who had heard the clamour and come out to see what was going on.

Jean-Claude called the owners, who came out the next week to check. Two saucepans and an electric fire had gone missing. Astonishingly, two years later the culprits were caught when they attempted to steal a ladder from a garden in a town several kilometres away and their fingerprints matched those of the saucepan thieves.

In the restaurant that night, we discussed how different it was in the UK, where reporting a crime merely seemed to result in being given a number to make an insurance claim. We waited an age for the crazy absinthe-drinking barman to bring the apéritifs we'd ordered: Kir for the ladies, beer for the men. He had come swaying over to the table to take our drinks order but appeared to have completely forgotten we were there and was absent-mindedly sipping from his topped-up glass of absinthe and staring into space.

We eyed the menu with little enthusiasm. Medallion of pork in Maroilles, a very smelly regional cheese, utterly delicious but not for everyone, and as Mark has an allergy to cheese, I tend to avoid it as he complains about the smell. Steak tartare, much loved by the French but completely baffling to foreigners. *Potjevleesch*, a regional speciality consisting of cold meat in aspic — usually rabbit, pork and chicken and a lot of yellowish jelly. The final choice was confit of duck.

Eventually, Monsieur Mad came over with

the drinks, spilling half on the way and thumping the glasses down on the table as if he thought the surface was a lot further away than it was.

'I'll try the potjevleesch,' said Karen gamely.

'*Potjevleesch* is off,' came the reply.

'I'll try the steak tartare,' said Joe. 'I'm up for a laugh.'

'No steak tartare,' the barman growled.

'*Porc an Maroilles?*' I asked.

'Non.'

So four confit de canard then. A famous stew of beans and duck pieces that is supposed to be a classic stalwart of great French cuisine.

'I don't think it's going to be good,' I said, 'but, if we're lucky, the boulangerie will still be open on the way home and I'll get us a cake.'

You can almost always rely on getting something to eat from a boulangerie when everything else is shut, at least during the day.

That day, in that restaurant, we were served what was, without a doubt, the worst, most unappetizing confit de canard I have ever seen in my life. It had clearly come out of a tin and had been briefly introduced to the oven. It was lukewarm, barely stirred and the duck fat was still hard, as was the bread that came with it.

Our friends from London loved the experience and dined out on the story for weeks after. We left the meal, paid the bill and wished the mad barman a happy new year and departed laughing.

The boulangerie was open and as luck would have it there was still some bread and a few cakes to be had, including *doigts de Charles Quint*, two long sponge fingers glued together with a bright red jam that oozed out and down the sides, topped with tiny slithers of green crystallized fruit.

'Fingers of Charles the Fifth,' explained the baker. 'He was the Holy Roman Emperor who ruled Spain and quite a bit of France including the Seven Valleys in the sixteenth century.' It turns out that the emperor had very bad gout and, despite making thousands of enemies, he didn't die in battle but of the disease. Someone cut off one of his hideous gouty old fingers to keep as a relic and, to this day, cakes are made in honour of it. Only in France.

Where we live, you wouldn't even know it was Christmas until maybe the week before, when the mayor organizes for the single string of lights that hangs all year round in a tree outside the town hall to be switched on.

You may see a few illuminations in a

174

window if you're lucky, perhaps a wreath of holly and mistletoe on a front door, cut from bushes and trees on the frosty country roads. The most obvious sign that it's that time of the year are the swinging Santas, horrible inflatable plastic Father Christmas figures climbing ropes or plastic ladders. They are tied to chimneys and gutters, swings and doorways, windows and gates. On a dark night, they're really quite creepy, a bit like festive peeping toms. On a windy day they sway back and forth, holding on to the rope for dear life or else are blown away to burst on a hawthorn bush.

This being France, a celebration involving copious amounts of food is what's really on everyone's mind. For me it has meant changing London habits, which used to consist of a mad dash to the supermarket on Christmas Eve to buy food for Christmas dinner. A fraught few hours in which the trolley would be stacked with packets and boxes, a long queue at the till, an even longer queue to get out of the car park. Here, I've learned to enjoy taking care over the planning, buying and cooking of the festive fayre.

At this time of year in France, you can quite easily eat yourself to a standstill.

It's become a tradition of ours to head to

the village of Licques in December, which is known locally as 'Turkey Town'. Here, a strange event takes place annually called La Fête de la Dinde, the Festival of the Turkey. The birds were introduced by monks at the local abbey in the seventeenth century and they've been bred there ever since, alongside Licques chickens, which feature on the menus of the best restaurants in France.

Almost anything seems to be an excuse for a party in northern France and this quirky turkey fiesta is certainly fun and festive. Go on the middle Sunday of December if you want to get a bird's-eye view of a unique spectacle. At one end of the rue Principale, an enormous cauldron the size of a small shed steams gently. A man has to climb a ladder to a long paddle that reaches into the cauldron's depths to stir the alcoholic drink that's boiled in the pot. It's a speciality of the town and its aim is to thaw out the hardy souls who brave the cold. I can vouch for the fact that it certainly gives you a warm glow. Next to the pot, about a hundred turkeys are hemmed in a pen, gobbling and flapping for all they are worth. Speeches are made (of course) and at about 11 a.m. (this being France it never quite starts on time) a parade takes place. The local food guild members are garbed in costumes that define their speciality: the Brotherhood of the Pomme de Terre in hessian sacks, the Brotherhood of the Chou-fleur with green hats. Local dignitaries, dressed in their formal robes, smile and nod to the crowds while a band plays stirring if not tuneful music. It's good humoured and great fun, but what we are all really here for is to see the turkeys escape.

'They rampage through the streets,' said Jean-Claude when he told me that the secret to a great Christmas dinner was to make sure that you went to the right places to get supplies, Licques being one of them.

Actually, what happens is the birds are let out, they amble leisurely up the street at their own pace, gently herded by a gaggle of children dressed in medieval costume. As thanks for their service, these turkeys escape being offered up as Christmas dinner.

Afterwards everyone goes to enjoy a lunch in a huge tent that seats a thousand people, with the central space cleared for dancing. Afterwards, it's time for shopping in a massive marquee. Foie gras, champagne, escargots, charpons (castrated cockerels), cheeses, baby Jesus sweets, St Nicolas biscuits, regional wines and a whole lot more — this gourmet market is where many of the locals go to taste and to buy specialities from all across France.

Bars and restaurants may sell more champagne in the run-up to Christmas, they may even put on a different menu, but on the whole here in the sticks, it's not a big commercial affair and life carries on pretty much as normal.

16

Animal magic

After dad died, we worked long hours renovating the house and growing vegetables. He wasn't rich by any stretch of the imagination but he left me enough money to pay off the mortgage on the French house. We built my dream kitchen from scratch. I went through old *Homes & Antiques* magazines showing Mark what I liked, including an article that featured Sir Terence Conran's kitchen in his south of France home. Mark drew pictures of cupboards and shelves and sketched what he thought I wanted. We built everything ourselves, including a lovely pantry cupboard made from the staircase we'd ripped out. Nothing was wasted if we could help it and we recycled where possible. A builder friend had been restoring a site belonging to the Ministry of Defence in London — where Winston Churchill had once had offices in the 1940s — and he told us a load of wood had been removed and was to go to the rubbish dump. We asked if we could have it; sure, they said, and we brought it out to France and stored it until we were ready to use it years later. When we eventually sanded the filthy thick wooden planks we found they were beautiful old oak floorboards. We made them into a staircase and I often think how I might be walking in the footsteps of the great man.

More boxes were unpacked as more rooms were finished, and in one of the boxes I came across the envelope with a chicken picture that my colleagues had given me when I left my job. It had been packed away for over two years, and when I opened it I found that my lovely friends had put money in it with a note saying it was to buy chickens with. We decided the time had come to honour their gift. We built a chicken coop and shelter at the bottom of the garden, ready for birds.

From spring through to autumn you can buy chickens of all sorts at street markets, of which there are many in this part of France. We headed to the Thursday morning market at Hesdin, which is a lively one that spreads from the main square in front of the town hall, down ancient cobblestone side roads, alongside the little canal that winds through the town and past the church.

A long line of cages filled with birds offered a confusion of choice, although for me it was more a question of did I like the look of them than what breed they were.

'Do you want to eat them?' asked Madame, who was selling them.

'God, no. We just want them for eggs,' I said, much to her amusement. City slickers playing at being country folk, I am sure she must have thought. But she took pity on us and picked out two brown, two white, two black and threw in a scrawny grey one for free.

The skinny grey bird grew rapidly, so much so that I began to think I had a special way with chickens. I called her Eaglet, as she resembled a baby eagle, all legs and sparse feathers. As the smallest in the group she got picked on so I gave her more attention than the rest. Eventually, she towered over the other girls and they all overcame their differences and got on well together. Every day Eaglet climbed into the nest box to lay an egg, as did all the birds. The strange thing was, even though I had seven chickens, there were only ever six eggs. Eaglet was an affectionate bird, eating out of my hands and cooing when I came to the pen. As she followed me everywhere and returned to the pen when I told her to, I carried on giving her special treatment and the run of the garden when I was out there.

One day I was hanging out the washing

when I heard a very loud cock-a-doodle-doo close by. I turned to see where the noise had come from. Eaglet turned too, looking behind her. There was nothing there, so I assumed it was one of my neighbour Claudette's birds. When I heard it again, the sound came from right by my feet. It was clear that the culprit was Eaglet. When I asked Jean-Claude if it was possible for chickens to sound like roosters and told him about Eaglet, he laughed so hard he almost choked.

She was, in fact, a he. I was not a champion chicken grower after all. Despite this, Eaglet continued to climb into the nest box every day like the girls and emerge a short while later making triumphant clucks

One day Eaglet broke his leg. I had grown very fond of him and didn't want him to suffer. I thought about taking him to the vet, but Jean-Claude assured me that it wasn't kind to prolong the agony and that it was time to learn how to deal with a sick bird and put it out of its misery. I couldn't do it; the duty fell to Mark, who hated every moment but accepted that it was something that had to be done.

'You really should eat him,' said Jean-Claude sensibly, and there was a part of me that agreed that we ought at least to try to live up to our self-sufficiency ambitions. So Mark despatched and plucked poor Eaglet and I cooked a coq au vin.

It smelled delicious in the slow cooker. It looked tempting on the plate. Mark tasted it gingerly and declared it disgusting. It was the excuse we needed; neither of our hearts were in it.

Later Jean-Claude popped by to see how it had gone and told us off for not trying harder. 'It's all in your head,' he remonstrated. 'That's why I told you not to give your birds a name.' It didn't matter, we knew we were pathetic but we also knew we would never eat one of our birds again — we were still townies at heart.

One Sunday morning we went to a flea market at Montcavrel, a hamlet close to Montreuil-sur-Mer. It was once an important place owned by grand lords of Picardy. Peter the Great, Tsar of Russia, stayed in a castle there in 1717, but sadly there are just two towers remaining of the once grand château. There is a smaller château whose claim to fame is that French King Louis Philippe spent a night there while on the run after abdicating.

Today it is a sleepy place with pretty front gardens and empty little roads, though on this Sunday the roads were thronging with stalls and people had come from far and wide to peruse the second-hand goods on sale.

There was a stall with a sign that read: 'Cockerel Nagasaki 5 euros'.

Mark and I looked at each other.

'No,' I said. 'We can't . . . we've got more than enough animals and we don't do well with cockerels.' I still missed Eaglet.

'Nagasaki, though,' said Mark, who is into martial arts and all things Japanese, and then, 'Five euros.' He does love a bargain.

So I spoke to the lady selling him, but she knew nothing about birds. She texted her husband who was in their house, behind the stall, and he duly arrived with their four children and a couple of friends.

I told him that we were thinking of getting a cockerel for our younger chickens, nine white birds we had recently added to our flock, which were very docile and sweet natured. They lived in a new pen and had never been near a cockerel.

By now everyone else in the road who was near enough to hear us talk, those who were selling or browsing, had stopped to watch.

'No problem,' said Monsieur the cockerel seller. 'Keep him in a separate bit of the pen where they can get to know each other but only through the fence. After a week let them be together and they'll sort it out.' He hesitated and then added, 'He is a lovely bird, but a little nervous.'

A crowd had gathered round by now.

After a bit more chat and advice we agreed to take the Nagasaki cockerel home and the wife of the seller procured a cardboard box.

Everyone seemed to take a step back.

The man bent down to get the cockerel out of the cage and I heard him say to the wife, 'Be careful, this bird is a right bastard.'

I looked at Mark — he hadn't heard . . . perhaps I was mistaken?

The cockerel was furious at being disturbed and put in a box: he squawked, screamed, pecked, flapped his wings, head-butted the sides and was generally quite mad — they had to use so much sticky tape to keep the lid down you could hardly see the cardboard. Luckily, we only live fifteen minutes away so we knew the bird would be all right with the few holes that we'd poked through, but it was clear *we* wouldn't be if he got out in the car on the way home.

I handed over 5 euros and we walked down the road with our box. Everyone was looking, which was hardly surprising after the commotion that the bird had made.

'Do you get the feeling that everyone is watching the crazy English pair who've just bought the most vicious, mentally disturbed, troublesome cockerel that ever lived?' I asked Mark.

I actually felt like people were waiting to applaud us.

On the way home I could feel the cockerel pecking the side of the box — I've never known a bird quite so determined to get out. They're normally really quiet in the dark and I talk to them to keep them calm. Not this one. Talking to him seemed to drive him wild.

We got him home and put him in a small pen on his own with some food and water.

Within two minutes he managed to wriggle through the fence into the older chickens' pen, the first set of birds we'd bought, which by now were quite grown up and had become very confident.

It seems he was a lot smaller than we'd realized.

The bullies were on him straight away — indignant and disgusted to have a man in their midst. Mark ran into the pen to catch him, but they cornered the cockerel and started to torment him. He then escaped into the field at the bottom of the garden.

Mark leaped over the fence and into the field on the other side. Usually there are cows grazing there, but not today — they had left plenty of reminders of their presence, however, which Mark trod in as he ran around in pursuit, risking a broken ankle thanks to the presence of many deep mole holes.

Watching Mark clutching a butterfly net, with which he hoped to catch the very sprightly young cockerel, and cursing when he had breath was the best entertainment I'd had in a while. Luckily for him, this being a Sunday afternoon, all the neighbours were enjoying a long leisurely lunch or I'm sure they'd have come out to watch.

Eventually, the cockerel ran into the little *chemin* at the side of the field, which leads to the road to the village one way and into hundreds of acres of fields the other way. Mark yelled at me to run round to the front of the alley so we could corner him.

I went as fast as I could, down the garden, through the house, down the road, into the *chemin* — there was no sign of Mark or the bird. As I stood there trying to get my breath back, I was pretty sure we would never see the cockerel again, when Mark appeared — a small dot in the distance — way across the fields. He was holding something . . .

We took the bird back to the garden and this time put him in a cage with smaller mesh next to the young chickens, and there he stayed for a few weeks, growing and crowing for all he was worth until he was too big to get through the fence in the big pen. We called him Kendo after Kendo Nagasaki, the British champion wrestler who was very famous in the 1970s. He is a beautiful bird with golden feathers and comes and goes at will, as he can climb fences with ease.

The birds had a surprising friend. 'Enry Cooper (named after the British heavyweight boxer) was a grey and white kitten with eye markings that made him look like a cute racoon. A malnourished stray, he simply walked through our open back door one day and decided we would be his family. He loved it in the chicken pen where the girls would fuss over him, inspecting him and giving him little affectionate pecks. In return he offered to chase them about a bit but not be mean to them.

Often I couldn't find him anywhere and he'd ignore my calls. One day I was late collecting the day's eggs. Opening the door to the nest box I discovered 'Enry Cooper sleeping in the warm straw. He stretched lazily and narrowed his eyes while I felt furtively underneath him for eggs. Amazingly, they were all safe. When I shut the door, the cat went back to sleep. We call him the chicken enforcer.

17

The Forrest Gump of blogging

The envelope containing the money and the picture of a chicken also bore a message from my friends: 'For chickens, because we think you're like *The Good Life*'.

I laughed when I read it. *The Good Life* was a 1970s British sitcom about a couple from Surbiton in southwest London who hankered after a rural life. A mid-life crisis saw them attempt to escape their city lifestyle, shun commercial values and become totally self-sufficient, growing vegetables and breeding chickens in their suburban garden. The series was incredibly popular in Britain and aired in the US as *Good Neighbors*.

The Good Life indeed, I thought to myself as, not wanting to make direct contact, I picked up a mouse nest on the end of a stick while we worked on renovating the utility room.

Later that night, when the third friend in a day phoned to get an update on how the work was going on the house, to find out if my tomato seeds had grown, if we'd frozen to death yet and how had my French onion soup turned out, the phrase on the message came to mind.

'We're *The Good Life* in France apparently,' I said to Mark, who was still trying to fit a window in the hall even though it was pitch black outside and pouring with rain. It was late but it couldn't be left or we'd be open to the elements all night.

'Living the dream,' he said as he hit his thumb with a hammer. 'Pass me that squirty foam, we're nearly there, just got to fill the gaps,' he called, just as the phone rang again. 'You should just send out a mail shot so they stop bloody ringing every night,' he said in annoyance. 'It's crazy — you're telling people the same stuff over and over again.'

How they laughed when I told them I'd somehow broken my finger carrying heavy bricks. The fact that I broke my toe dropping a gas bottle on my foot filled them with mirth. But they also wanted to know if my hours of planting vegetable seeds was worth it and whether Jean-Claude, my lovely French neighbour who had become my mentor, had been proved right when he advised me to plant according to the moon's waxing and waning . . . and how was the laying of floors coming along, and had I learned to cook yet?

'Perhaps I should start a 'The Good Life

France' page on Facebook,' I ventured, 'or maybe a blog?'

'Blog? You do know that means you'd need a website,' sniggered Mark. 'You're the least techy person I've ever met in my life. How would you create a website and put stuff on it?'

He was right: I was and still am a technophobe. But the seed of an idea had been planted in my head, and my dad's words, 'you should write', returned to me over and over.

When the phone continued to ring regularly I brought the subject up again with Mark.

'I really like the idea of The Good Life France blog,' I said. 'It means I could keep in touch with my friends and family every day and gives me a chance to start writing again.' Years before I'd worked as a writer on a glossy magazine in London and loved it but gave it up because the hours weren't great for a single mum.

Although I was a disaster when it came to anything technical, Mark wasn't and had been studying how to build websites. We had anticipated that Mark would carry on working as a financial advisor after we moved to France, but we hadn't realized just how long the recession would last and how much the finance industry would change. Work was hard to come by.

Mark had been training for a new career. A great salesman already, he had learned how to write computer languages, how to design and build websites and was planning to start a business making websites. I could be his first client, I told him.

I drew a picture of what I thought a homepage should look like. Mark set up a website reflecting what he thought I should have. We wrestled over the look, the feel. 'I don't want to be corporate,' I told him. 'It's not me any more. I want it to be friendly and fun and fabulous. Where I can share what I learn: real life in France.'

By this time, I had started to be the go-to expat for other expats in the area. People would ring or turn up at our house to ask for help with their paperwork, to find out how to locate a tax office, where the rubbish dump was, who to sell their house with, what was a good language course for expats with not much time and a hundred other questions. It was a great way of meeting other expats in the area and I learned a lot about the sort of problems people encountered when buying in or moving to France.

I decided to include practical advice pieces on my website. From there it was an easy decision to write about everything anyone would ever want to know about France.

Even though I didn't really have much of a clue what Hogging or a blog was, I was excited about having one. At the very end of 2011, I wrote my first post. I typed it and emailed it to Mark because I had no idea how to put it on the website he'd designed. I sent him a photo separately to go with it. He uploaded it to www.thegoodlifefrance.com — my new website. I wrote a few more posts and sent them to Mark to upload.

A friend set up a Twitter page for me as I had never even looked at Twitter. Mark set up a Facebook page for The Good Life France as I was so clueless.

Twenty-five of my friends liked my Facebook page and followed my Twitter account and I shared my posts with them.

It was fun.

After a month I checked the stats — 480 people had looked at my website.

I was absolutely delighted and very surprised. My friends had shared my posts with their friends.

I wrote another post about my life in France and one about how to get electricity set up and a few other items I thought might be interesting. I wrote them and emailed them to Mark, who is not a patient man, so, by the end of five weeks I learned how to upload my own posts and photos. Mark calls me the Forrest Gump of blogging — once I started, I didn't stop.

At the end of six months I checked the stats again: sixty thousand people had looked at my website.

I was ecstatic.

I was also completely and utterly hooked.

I'd hardly used Facebook before I went to France but now I loved sharing news and photos of life here, the places I visited and the things I saw, the food I ate. I gained new friends from around the world, Lori from Georgia, Julia from New Zealand, Fred from France and many others. This is interesting, I thought: I'm sitting here in my little French farmhouse in the middle of nowhere talking to people all around the world about my life!

A year in and I had five hundred friends on Facebook — I was amazed. It had a profound effect. There were certainly times when I felt quite lonely in my new life. Although there was always a lot to be done, it was usually just the two of us and I could go whole days without seeing someone other than Mark. When he was away working in London on his website development business, it was just me on my own a lot of the time, but with Facebook I could 'talk' to people pretty much any time of the day.

My new friends from around the world started to ask me questions about France. They wanted practical advice like what bank did I think was good for expats or how to get a phone installed in their new French home. Others wanted to know what restaurants I recommended locally and elsewhere in France, and those following the page would add their tips too; it began to feel like a community. One expat woman who spoke little French and had just opened a gîte wrote in a panic saying that her French guests had emailed to ask if it was okay if they brought their shepherd with them — he was from Germany. She only had one room free and couldn't accommodate an extra person, but she wasn't sure if she'd read their email right. I told her to send it to me and I'd see if I could help. I could — they wanted to bring their dog, a berger allemand, a German Shepherd!

I posted something on my Facebook page every day, photos of things I saw, like cakes in the local patisseries or the markets I visited, and by the end of the next year I had five thousand Facebook friends — I was completely astonished. It inspired me to share more photos and tips about travel and life in France generally; other people started to share their photos and recommendations on my Facebook page too, and my circle of amies and amis grew and grew, reaching more than a hundred thousand. I was truly humbled, and utterly thrilled.

I think of most of them as friends I haven't met, and I know we share at least one common interest — France. I say most of them because I actually have met quite a few people I never would have without my Facebook page. One day I posted that I was trying to make curtains for the house and I was really struggling. I bought some material on eBay at a knockdown price and had to make twenty-five pairs of curtains. Although I had a sewing machine my mother-in-law had given me, I had no idea how it worked and I was doing all the sewing by hand. A woman commented on the post saying she thought she lived near me and she would help me to learn how to use my sewing machine. She turned out to be an expert quilt maker who lived about 8 kilometres away, and she spent several hours patiently taking me through the processes of sewing-machinery and we became friends. I've now met people from all around the world via Facebook, like Susan from Tennessee who was Dolly Parton's glass maker (who has a glass maker?!). Sometimes I would post a photo of somewhere I was visiting and people would share their tips and photos. I was learning more about France from Facebook than I'd ever thought possible.

By now publishers were sending me books about France and asking me to review them for the website. When I finished a book I popped the review on Facebook and did a random draw for anyone who said they'd like the copy. An Australian woman called Carolyn won one of the books and told me she saw it as fate. For years she had longed to have a French adventure and winning the book prompted her to take action. She joined a tour to Paris and Provence and by good luck I was in Paris on one of the days she was there. We met at the gorgeous Treize bakery in Saint-Germain-des-Prés, run by expat American Laurel Sanderson. It is tucked away in a courtyard opposite the Hotel da Vinci, so named after the *Mona Lisa* was hidden there on the top floor by a thief who stole it from the Louvre in 1911. Carolyn and I recognized each other immediately from our Facebook photos, and didn't feel like strangers at all.

Fred from France has become a great friend over the years and often helps me with tricky French questions. Coincidentally, his grandfather was born in my little village; he knows the area intimately and really understands the sense of humour of its inhabitants. When I'm unsure if Jean-Claude is teasing me, I'll ask Fred! Although we've only met in person once, we've become real friends.

I was starting to receive invitations to visit different regions so that I could write about my trip, and what had started as a hobby became an all-encompassing affair.

Ernest Hemingway once said, 'Writing and travel broaden your arse if not your mind.' He was right and that was okay by me; I had found my passion (though I have to diet a lot these days).

18

Tour de France

In a town where not very much happens, to have the Tour de France come through is a bit of a coup.

So it was that, in the summer of 2014, one of the biggest sporting events on earth was welcomed to Hucqueliers, close to where I live. In the Middle Ages it was an important village where a grand château once stood opposite the fifteenth-century church, which still remains. It seems that the locals objected to one of Louis XIV's taxes, imposed to pay for the guarding of the borders with Spanish territory a little to the north. The peasants of Hucqueliers and nearby Desvres and Marquise rebelled. The King's Lieutenant in Picardy brought his cannons to Hucqueliers and took pot-shots at the château and destroyed both it and the rebellion. Ever since, Hucqueliers has been a tranquil farming community. It is now home to about five hundred inhabitants, a boulangerie, a couple of friendly bars — including my regular — a restaurant and a handful of shops. It's a popular meeting place for hikers because of the glorious countryside that surrounds it.

On the day that the circus that is the Tour de France came to town, Hucqueliers was mobbed. Thousands arrived from all around and from further afield. Mad (but fit) Brits hopped on a ferry from Dover and cycled 96 kilometres to Hucqueliers to join in the celebration. Mayors from villages for miles around arrived wearing their best suits to take their place in history. Photographers from the local paper were there to capture the moment for posterity.

I arrived an hour before the race was due to pass through and positioned myself to take photos of the cyclists coming down one steep hill, past the ancient church and into the sharp corner that would carry them up another challenging hill and out of sight.

Opposite my post, an elderly man sat in a chair smiling and waving a small flag; young girls hung out of windows holding camera phones to take pictures to send to their friends. Amazingly, the sun shone — this being the north you can never guarantee such a thing even in summer. The atmosphere was electric, everyone was happy. Or so it seemed.

Ten minutes in and I could hear a tone of misery as a woman walked past muttering 'merde'. It wasn't an isolated incident; more people walked past moaning, looking unhappy. Had they heard something awful? Had the Tour been diverted? I wandered down the hill to where the mayors and councillors were, but they still looked pleased as punch. The only auberge in town was doing roaring business. Across the road, though, I heard a few moans and groans of 'oh la la la la' (there are more la la's when something is particularly bad or particularly good) and 'merde'. They were coming from outside the boulangerie. What on earth was going on?

I drifted across the road, narrowly missing two young men dressed from head to toe in red, white and blue silk, faces painted in the same colours, arms linked, singing the Marseillaise and lurching from side to side. The sole gendarme, there to control the huge crowds single-handedly, attempted to move them on, much to the amusement of the onlookers.

As soon as I got to the door of the bakery I could see what the problem was. It was shut. But it was meant to be open and that, it seems, was enough to ruin the day for some of the people there. You see, a Frenchman must have his bread. It is the law. No, I'm not kidding, it really is the law. Or at least it was until very recently.

In 1790, a law was passed that decreed that bakers must declare the date of their holidays to the mayor in order that he could approve or veto the dates and thereby ensure that not all bakers took their holidays at the same time because that might mean no bread for the people and, as you know, not having enough bread in those days was enough to cause a revolution. However, in an effort to eradicate red tape in the twenty-first century, apparently, bakers can now take their holiday when they want, and if that means that all the bakers go away at the same time — then so be it. Off to the supermarket to buy hideous, mass produced, half baked, disgusting little bread sticks to finish baking at home. In 1790, the person who made that decision might well have paid with his head. The presidential candidate who promises to overrule this so-called progression might well get into power on that alone — my French friends are aghast at such a stupid idea that impacts their ability to get bread whenever they want or need it. In reality, there is usually a boulangerie open when you need one — even on Christmas Day you can generally find one open so that you can get your fresh bread fix.

Back in Hucqueliers, the baker had been baking like mad all morning. He had baked as fast as he dared. He had been tireless in his efforts to bake enough bread for the hordes that were expected. He failed. By midday the bread had all gone, the cakes had gone — the shop was empty. The baker closed the door and stepped outside. He wanted to see the riders go past and refused to return to the kitchen until they had.

Of course, for the locals this was a catastrophe of the highest order, and I suspect that there are more than a few from that momentous day in Hucqueliers who remember it not for the razzmatazz or the giant papier mâché horse that a tractor towed into town (I'm not quite sure why). They won't reminisce about the children who wore their special T-shirts and learned a song and dance routine to honour the riders who whizzed through so quickly the kids never even got to the end of the first chorus. They won't recollect the thousands of people who were smiling and happy or the decorated trucks from which corporate gifts were chucked. They won't recall the sight of the old man who was hit with a bottle of water thrown from one of the parade vehicles and ran into the road ranting and shaking his fists only to get hit on the head with a Madeleine cake.

They remember it as the historic day that

Hucqueliers ran out of bread.

Desvres, one of the towns that rebelled against the Sun King's hated taxes, is a short drive from Hucqueliers and is where the famous Desvres pottery has been made since the 1700s. It is a great place to visit on a Tuesday morning when the town square comes to life with a street market. Afterwards we always head to a little bar outside of which is a cardboard cut-out of a buxom barmaid that certainly caught my dad's attention when we first went to the town. Inside it is like stepping over the threshold of time to discover you have arrived in the 1950s. There are almost always a couple of old men sitting at the bar nursing their glasses of pastis as though the miracle of youth is to be found in the bottom of the pale liquid. The wallpaper and furnishings are most definitely mid-twentieth-century vintage, dark brown and orange swirls — think LSD meets a kaleidoscope. A canary in a cage is in a different location each time you visit, sometimes on the pool table, sometimes on the bar, on the windowsill or the floor near the door if it's a fine day. This place feels as though nothing has changed for decades. The elderly barmaid, who could not be more different from the enticing sign outside, serves coffee at the pace of a snail. Her yappy dog attempts to either nip or hump the legs of strangers. We have grown to love this place for what it is: quirky, weird and very French.

One day we went in and Madame the barmaid was chatting coquettishly with an old man at the bar.

'I was the toast of the Folies Bergère in my day,' she said in her hoarse, hundred-cigarettes-a-day voice. 'When I did the splits, the crowd would gasp.' She took a big wheezy breath and fixed her eyes on him. 'My breasts were like cushions from heaven.'

The old man brushed a hand across his rheumy eyes as if he could almost see the pillowy mounds. He tapped his empty pastis glass on the counter for more. The barmaid never took her eyes off him, but reached an arm out to one side, grasped a bottle and filled his glass.

'I could have had anyone I wanted. Maurice Chevalier wouldn't leave me alone, you know. Every night my dressing table was full of flowers.' She paused and sighed and looked around the bar, seeing me listening, all agog.

She leaned in confidentially towards the elderly customer. 'You know, I can still do the splits, if you want to see?' and she winked lasciviously, causing the man to snort and then down his pastis in one go.

They don't do pubs in France. Of course, in London I was spoiled by a plethora of pubs. There's something about the aroma of beer, the sticky carpets, wooden bars with their smelly towels to mop up the spilt alcohol, dim lights and the promise of a good night. A bar in France just isn't the same.

For a start, in my area, they're very friendly to strangers. The first time we walked into our local bar in Hucqueliers, the conversation stopped dead and everyone turned to look at us. I stood frozen to the spot at this unexpected reaction, and was amazed when, one by one, every person there nodded to us and said, 'Monsieur, madame,' to acknowledge our arrival then carried on where they'd left off.

We sat at a table and the man behind the bar came over to take our orders and shake our hands.

'Ah,' he said, 'you're the new English lot from down by Embry, aren't you?'

It was our first full weekend in our new house. I'd heard the country grapevine was rife here but I was impressed by how fast news spread — it was certainly better than the BBC.

That night, when customers left they shook hands with everyone, including us. It was our first experience of the legendary friendliness of the people of the Seven Valleys.

It took an age for me to get used to the fact that some of my neighbours do not always find it necessary to knock at the front door. They are quite happy to wander round the back of the house and into the garden. Some are even happy to just walk in through the front door if it is open. Our water meter is in a well inside the house and one day the meter reader simply walked straight in while we were eating lunch, said 'bonjour', walked over to the well, lifted up the lid, read the meter and walked back out.

There have been times when I have spotted a farmer driving his tractor very slowly at the bottom of our garden peering over the fence to see what the mad English have been up to in the garden.

When we were replacing windows in the front of the house, our tiny little road that leads to nowhere became the most popular place for a promenade in the whole village. The local builder in our village drove past in his van on his way home each lunch time to see how far we'd got. Claudette sometimes went by shaking her head in astonishment, and Jean-Claude later told us that she berated him for his slowness since she had noted that we were able to fit three roof windows in a single day, therefore why had it taken him three weeks to do a single window?

It is not possible to keep secrets in a village like this — everyone knows your business. I can't really complain, though, since my life and the people who feature in it are the subject of my writing.

19

French cuisine

This part of northern France is not known for its haute cuisine, and yet here is the vegetable garden of France: Boulogne-sur-Mer is the country's biggest fresh fish processing centre, and the rich soil provides fine fodder for livestock. Local dishes tend to be rather hearty in winter months as you'd expect, and the ubiquitous moules et frites is as popular here as in almost every region of France.

Typical menu stalwarts are *carbonnade flamande* (a beef stew made with brown sugar and beer), *flammekueche* (a sort of thin pizza made with crème fraîche) and tarts made with local cheese. And this area has some particularly smelly cheeses. One, called Vieux-Boulogne, was tested by scientists at Oxford University and came top of the stinkiest cheese in the world list. Maroilles is another with a mighty powerful aroma, created by Benedictine monks in the tenth century in the eponymous town. It is soaked in locally produced beer and is a staple of dishes throughout the north of France. I once ordered a tart smothered in melted Maroilles in a restaurant in Lille and got a round of applause from the French customers — they are very proud of their cuisine here.

There is, though, one thing that really puzzled me when I first arrived — chips, fries, or frites as they call them in France. Frites vans and frites shops are everywhere in this part of the country, more so than in any other region I've been to. On a through road between Hucqueliers and Hennoville, a resident decided to set up a frites van in his front garden. Friterie Francky now attracts people from far and wide. When he is open for business he turns on orange flashing lights on his gate posts, and you can be sure that the road outside will be chock-a-block with cars arriving for their frites fix. He has even turned an outbuilding into a dining area, and plays great music in the courtyard, which is a meeting place over a plate of frites for expats and locals on Friday and Saturday nights. Regulars are greeted with a kiss on the cheek from Francky and Arnaud who works with him, and people don't seem to mind going home with the wrong order, as happens from time to time. You can of course have all manner of side orders with your frites, from dressed crab to a glass of red wine. It might just be chips, but this is France after all!

Since we had no oven in the house when we first came here — at least not one we ever learned how to use as it ran on coal and only ever filled the house with smoke — we cooked on a barbecue, had chips from Francky's or enjoyed baguettes with an accompaniment. There isn't much that will beat a freshly baked baguette from the boulangerie, a hunk of cheese from the fromagerie, some fresh tomatoes from the marché and a cake from the pâtisserie.

'Food of the Gods,' my dad used to say.

Whether it was raining and cold, or sunny and warm, we have never got fed up with this simple fare and have learned to truly appreciate seasonal, local, fresh produce.

The French are a nation of hunter-gatherers. When you drive around the countryside you'll see them at the side of the roads, picking berries, apples, wild garlic or mushrooms. Once I was driving home and passed a deer that had been hit by a car; the poor thing was quite dead. As I pulled into the village I mentioned it to Jean-Claude who was outside his garage nattering to a man in a tractor. I've never seen Jean-Claude move so fast — he was off like lightning, cutting short what had seemed to be an engrossing conversation and leaping into his little white van to retrieve the complimentary 'meal'.

Picking mushrooms is so popular that many chemists in France offer a free mushroom checking service. Not everyone cares to take precautions, though, and every year there are several deaths from eating poisonous ones. Nowadays there are fewer pharmacies offering the service than there used to be, perhaps because of the prevailing mood of health and safety and fear of prosecution. Although France is not any-where near the sue-for-a-peanut-league of America or the UK, this mindset is starting to creep in.

In the next village along, one of my British friends asked if I'd like to join her and her French neighbour Stefan in the woods for a few hours of mushroom picking. Of course, I said, it sounded like fun. Off we headed to the forest near Hesdin, which is an unusual little town with a fascinating history. The famous musketeer D'Artagnan learned to read and write here. Charles V's vast territory in the north ended at Hesdin and he built a palace there for his sister, Marie of Hungary; the Imperial Eagle of the Habsburgs is sculpted over the porch. Later the building became Hesdin's town hall when Philip II of Spain became ruler of the local areas of Flanders and Artois and the royal arms of

Spain are sculpted over the balcony.

In the forest where kings and noblemen once hunted we spent several hours mooching around mushroom mounds. Stefan, a real fun guy (oh, I can hear you groan at that!), had instructed us to bring a wicker basket so that the spores of the mushrooms we picked could fall through the holes — it helps propagation apparently. With his help, we managed to gather a sizeable collection of various colours. He invited us back to his house to check in his book of mushrooms to make sure that they were all safe.

Stefan lives in a small lane that is really just a dirt track on which ducks and chickens promenade, and his house looks neglected and derelict. The step that leads from the front door to the hall is covered in moss. Inside it was cold and damp and very dingy since the shutters were closed and the single light bulb would have been hard pushed to attract the smallest moth that ever lived. He seemed to inhabit one room that served all his needs except as a bathroom, which I didn't ask about after he boasted that his mattress was over a hundred years old.

The book in which Stefan checked our mushrooms was dated 1896 and was full of very poor drawings that could have been anything vaguely mushroomy. He held our bounty up, stared at them and then at the book intently, leafing pages, frowning and fondling the fungi. Clearing his throat he announced, 'They're all good. No problem with these. They will be delicious, gently sauteed in butter for your supper.'

My friend and I left and decided that just to be sure we'd pop to the pharmacy. Luckily, Monsieur the chemist was delighted to help and proclaimed himself a mushroom expert. Putting on his glasses he examined the little pile in our baskets, picking them up, mumbling and popping some to one side, others back in the basket. Each time we started to talk he glared at us; clearly this was a serious business, so we kept quiet. By the end of his investigation, he'd put all the mushrooms back in the basket except for one, a huge monster with a pointy hat that we thought was quite a prize.

'Are you married, Mesdames?' he asked. We both nodded.

'Are you both happily married?' he said, looking from one to the other.

'Yes,' we said.

'Why do you ask?' enquired my friend.

'Well, if you love your husbands, you should not feed them this one.' He pointed to our prize giant.

'Would it kill my husband if I gave him that

one?' asked my friend, going white at the thought.

'No,' said the pharmacist chortling, 'but he would shit for a week!'

Hunting is popular in my part of rural France, though often it's less about catching something to eat and more about an excuse to drink beer and socialize. In my village of just 142 people there are no fewer than seven hunting clubs as people keep falling out with each other, so they leave one club and start another. The most popular meeting space is an old Second World War German bunker in the forest close to our house where there was once a V1 launch site. The runway still remains, and there are plenty of traces left from the time when there was a huge camp there. The bunker is half buried in the moist forested ground and these days it's a popular place for local hunters to play cards when they're taking a break from hunter-gathering. Jean-Claude once asked Mark if he wanted to go along but hunting holds no appeal for either of us, though I did ask if I could go in the interests of research. Jean-Claude was completely horrified: a woman, going hunting? He was flabbergasted.

'Non' was the answer, although he did offer me the chance to go and help cook lunch with his wife and her friends, while the men were running about in the woods with guns attempting to despatch small animals and wild pigs.

Sometimes the hunting is not quite what you'd expect.

On a cool spring morning, Jean-Claude came to the house and said he needed to 'borrow' Mark for 'cinque minutes' and he mentioned something about a barrel, which neither of us understood. So Mark departed on the back of Jean-Claude's tractor, none the wiser about what was required, which is fairly normal.

An hour later he returned — he was ashen-faced and looked quite queasy.

He said he'd gone to Jean-Claude's barn where he keeps his ugly horse and stores food for his numerous rabbits, chickens, geese, pigeons and ducks. In all I think he has around 250 animals of one sort or another, but it may be much more as they're kept in different places around the village — his garden, his mother-in-law's garden and various fields — so it's hard to tell, and he has no idea himself.

As Mark doesn't speak much French and Jean-Claude speaks no English they resorted to charades and hand gestures. Jean-Claude asked Mark to fill a big barrel in the centre of the barn with water via a hosepipe lying next to it.

Mark looked inside the barrel to see half a dozen rats scurrying around in the bottom. Jean-Claude explained that he had a serious rat problem in the barn, which had to be controlled as it could be dangerous for him and his animals. They attack baby chickens, carry diseases and bite humans if scared. Not wanting to harm his animals by putting rat poison down, he'd run a wooden ramp up to the barrel, filled it with rat-tempting goodies, and of course once in they couldn't climb out. Jean-Claude said he hated rats so much he couldn't go near the barrel. Mark thought the idea of drowning a load of trapped rats was horrendous, unsporting and he didn't want to do it either. There was some discussion accompanied by much shuddering, many gestures and more face pulling. In the end they shared the job.

It was around this time that we realized that we would never be anything but fake country folk; the townie in us was just too strong.

20

More cats than you can shake a tail at

Something seems to happen to people when they become expats in France. I've seen it with my own eyes. It has to do with becoming crazy animal lovers.

I was introduced to a lovely couple called Gary and Annette from England. When French people find out that you're British, they want to tell you about every British person that they know in the area — they think they're helping but sometimes it isn't always so. Just because you're foreigners in France doesn't mean you'll get on with everyone else who's in the same boat.

Gary and Annette, though, are exceptional. They are funny, kind-natured and ever so slightly bonkers.

Annette keeps chickens, and not just a few. She tells me she started with five chicks from the local supermarket and got hooked rapidly, buying a couple more each time she went shopping. At certain times of the year in rural northern France, garden centres and even some supermarkets stock chicks, ducklings and goslings the same way that supermarkets in the UK stock seasonal plants. Fortunately, she has a large enough garden to accommodate them all comfortably.

Annette's chickens live side by side with ducks, geese, guinea fowl, quail, a large turkey, four cats, two dogs and two goats. Heidi and Gerty the goats are what you might kindly call entertaining. When Annette and Gary go away for a night I pop in to make sure the menagerie is okay and to feed them all, and every time it's always the goats that cause a problem. They are greedy, mean and, quite frankly, scary. They love to escape and cause mayhem.

Annette is very hands-on with her animals. One time, arriving at her house, I waded through the birds that live in the courtyard and knocked at the front door. Waiting an age, I was about to leave thinking she must be out when the door opened very slowly and Annette beckoned me in. She walked along her passageway with careful, deliberate steps and into the kitchen. All of her movements were hugely exaggerated and slow, as if she was in a bubble filled with treacle that at the slightest rash movement might burst. She sat down gingerly.

'Have you hurt yourself?' I asked.

'No,' she laughed. 'I've got an egg in my bra.'

It's hard to know what to say to that. It turns out that Annette, on her morning egg-gathering and chicken-checking rounds the day before, had discovered that one of the chickens that had been sitting on some duck eggs had given up. Annette checked the nest; all of the eggs were cold except one. When she picked it up and held it close to her ear, she could hear a 'cheep cheep' from inside. In a quandary, she says her first thoughts were, 'It needs somewhere warm. I know, I'll pop it in my bra.'

'I'm not sure that's what I would have thought of,' I told her as I made the tea in her unusual kitchen. Annette and Gary are hoarders of cups and saucers, bowls and pots, cookery books and kitchen paraphernalia. They love nothing more than to browse and bargain at flea markets and most weekends go home laden with things to re-love. As a result, their kitchen is filled to the rafters with this and that. You have to move something from a chair to sit, something from the oven to cook, and something from the table to make space to put down a cup of tea.

'Well,' went on Annette, justifying her actions, 'I remember as a kid we had chickens and if one of them abandoned an almost ready egg, my grandmother would pop the egg in a glove and put it on top of something warm like the oven. I was worried about roasting it, though.'

She told me that, the night before, she and Gary had gone to dinner at a friend's house. The egg went too. All through the meal Gary and Annette, who had not mentioned the additional dinner guest to their hosts, were trying to stifle their giggles as they could hear cheeping noises coming from her chest and their host kept removing his hearing aid and tapping it trying to locate the source of the noise.

The day after my visit, Annette phoned me to let me know the egg had hatched early that morning. She was sitting at the kitchen table with a mug of tea, when she felt a crack in her bra. The egg started to move about so she whipped it out and popped it on to the table. My friend watched, mesmerized, as a beak emerged through the shell, quickly followed by a fluffy yellow duckling.

Annette is now the proud mother of Titania, named after the Queen of the Fairies in *A Midsummer Night's Dream*, of course.

Another couple I know, Leanne and Mike, moved to the Dordogne area from the UK for health reasons. They like dogs — in fact, they had two that went with them. When one of their beloved pets died, they went to the SPA, the local animal refuge, to find the remaining dog a companion. They particularly wanted an older animal as their dog was getting on a bit. They were horrified to discover that old dogs were euthanized as it was so hard to re-home them. They ended up going home with seven dogs that day. Now they have up to thirty-five at any one time in their home. Many of the dogs are sick, almost all are very old and often don't live for a long time, requiring a lot of care. This couple somehow cope with the stress and sadness of constantly losing animals that they truly care for, many of them having been abused and neglected. Leanne and Mike call themselves The Twilight Retirement Home for Dogs and over the years they've gathered a group of like-minded friends who help them raise money to look after all the animals. They are not rich, just an ordinary retired couple surviving on a pension in France and living a quite extraordinary life with their much-loved pets.

I've met many people here in France who take in animals. They're not all retirees with time on their hands. I think that, like me, many of them feel that with a big garden and a bit more free time than they're used to, there's room for an animal or several in your life.

This is, of course, leading up to me telling you that we somehow ended up with fifteen ducks, two geese, four more chickens and another three cats about a year after 'Enry Cooper arrived.

Loulou came from a flea market. Some kids had her in a box and they were begging someone to take her as their mum wouldn't let them keep her. They spotted us suckers a mile off. I went home from that flea market with a bucket, a butter pat and a mewing tortoiseshell kitten.

Shadow was a jet black kitten who adopted Mark when we went to dinner with friends in another village. She kept sitting on his lap and wouldn't leave his side; our friends pleaded with us to take her as they had so many. When we went home, the kitten came with us.

Ginger Roger is a totally deaf ginger tom. He was starving and terrified of everything when I found him in the garden. However, he took an immediate shine to me and though he wouldn't come in the house, I made him a little hut outside and fed him every day. I did take him to the vet for a check-up and was told never to bring him back when he attacked the vet's assistant. It's not that he is a bad cat, but because he can't hear, he's terrified. 'I don't care,' said my vet. 'He's not a house cat, he's a wild cat and we can't help with this one.'

One morning I went down to the pens where the chickens and ducks happily cohabitate. As usual the seven ducklings, Sneezy, Wheezy, Grumpy, Nosey, Chewy, Sleepy and Beaky, had escaped and were following me about. At ten weeks old they had little of their yellow fluff left and were voraciously curious and hungry, and this lot were particularly tame. The parent ducks had been a gift from a neighbour. We knew nothing about keeping them but found out shortly after that they love nothing better than to eat, splash in a pond and hatch their eggs.

That morning, on my way out of the pen after feeding the noisy birds, I almost trod on a tiny duckling. It was lying on its side, its head floppy, not moving. I picked it up; its feet and beak were freezing cold and it was bleeding — it had clearly been pecked by some of the other birds. It is one of the horrible discoveries about keeping fowl. They are really not very nice at times. Sure, some of them have great personalities, they can be very cute and fun too, but they can also be aggressive and mean. They don't call it henpecked for nothing. I picked up the newly hatched duckling and cupped it in my hands to warm it. There was no sign of a mother to care for it and I was sure it would die in my hands. I could see the life ebbing away.

Mark had gone to the shops and I waited anxiously for him to return. He came back to find me in floods of tears in the kitchen with duckling poo on my hands and shirt. Calmly, he found a box, set up the heat lamp and put a jam jar lid of water in it. I popped the duckling in and it cheeped very feebly just once. I hugged Mark. It's one of the things I have discovered about him that I never knew before we came to France: he is just as soft as me when it comes to animals.

Then we walked round the pens and checked the hedges to see if there were any more ducklings. We found a hatched eggshell in the chicken coop and the mother duck still sitting on the other eggs. She'd been there the entire summer and nothing had happened. I'd thought about pushing her off but ended up just cleaning around her as she got so distressed. Clearly, this egg was ready ahead of time and she had decided to just stay in situ for the others, which meant checking the coop regularly from now on to see if we could catch any more. I had to set the alarm for sunrise, which is when most of the eggs tend to hatch.

Jean-Claude thinks that I am completely

and utterly crazy. Why try to save a duckling? You can buy them in the shops or at farms for a euro, and if you ask your neighbour nicely, you can get them for free.

Mark says to me, 'You can't save them all,' but I try and so far I've been very lucky, rarely losing any, except for one time when I took a few ducklings from a neighbour who didn't want them. Unfortunately, they brought a virus with them that wiped them all out and some of mine too.

Amazingly, by the afternoon the duckling was running about and cheeping away. I called him Rocky after the Sylvester Stallone film because this little one was obviously a survivor. He thought I was his mum and would go crazy every time he heard or saw me and I picked him up quite a bit so he wouldn't feel so alone. He grew to love sitting in a little box on my lap at night watching TV or dozing while I read a book. When he was three weeks old, a neighbour came to the rescue with another duckling so he would have company and learn how to interact with his peers. Within a few weeks the pair of them were integrated into the pen with the rest of the ducks. Rocky rushes to the gate when I go to feed them each day and loves to eat from my hands.

With five cats, two dogs and numerous

birds, almost all of them wanting some attention ranging from cuddles to a pat on the head, I really didn't want any more pets.

Let me tell you, living the dream with a small homestead involves a certain amount of stuff that is not that much fun and more of a nightmare than a dream, namely poo. The cats are good on the whole and spend most of their time outdoors, but on cold nights the girls like to stay in and that means a litter tray to deal with in the morning.

The dogs have their own run in the garden and that has to be cleared up.

The chickens, ducks and geese have five houses between them, all of which have to be cleaned. I shall never want for manure in the garden.

One dark November night we were driving home from the shops. We pulled into our little road and, by the bright glare of our headlights, saw a big black dog at the side of our neighbour Madame Jupe's house. It was bitterly cold, a harsh wind blew the trees wildly, the great balls of mistletoe that cling to the branches were swinging back and forth, icy sleet fell. It was a nasty night.

Even by our neighbours' standards, leaving a dog out in this sort of weather was bad. Generally, people here are less, shall we say, sentimental towards their animals than we are. Many dogs are kept in cages day and night; they are working dogs, not pets. Madame Jupe has a dog she loves very much, and though it spends all day tied to her front door, she lets it sleep in the house at the foot of the stairs every night.

We hoped the Jupes would soon take in what we thought was their new dog.

An hour later Mark went to look.

The dog was still there.

He went and checked four times and then came home and told me he simply couldn't stand the thought of the dog being out there in these conditions. He was going to knock on their door to see if they knew their poor animal was out there suffering; perhaps they had forgotten about it.

I went too as Monsieur Jupe never understands a word Mark says.

We knocked. Monsieur Jupe came to the door and opened it just a few inches and peered at us as if we were crazy people come to kidnap him and Madame.

'Oui?'

'Bonsoir, sorry to disturb you but we thought you ought to know your dog is outside.'

'My dog? No, my dog is inside sitting on Madame Jupe's lap in front of the fire!'

'No, we've just seen him, your new dog, the big black one.'

'Non, that's not our dog.' Monsieur Jupe opened the door a fraction more. 'That dog has been there for two weeks. He's got rabies. We are waiting for someone to take him away.'

With that he bid us a good night and closed the door against the howling wind.

'I can't leave that dog here all night,' said Mark, and we walked round to the side of the house.

The dog was enormous, with wild, staring eyes. As we approached, he slunk down low and backed up against the wall, growling. Slime hung out of his mouth and he was breathing fast and shaking.

'Don't go near him. He's got rabies,' I cautioned.

'That dog hasn't got rabies,' scoffed Mark. 'He's terrified and he's freezing. Go and get some rope.'

I ran back to the house thinking that, by the time I got back, Mark could have rabies too. I grabbed my thick gardening gloves (I am not sure what good I thought that would do) and the rope and ran back.

Mark was talking to the dog who was cowering against the wall; he put the rope gently over its head and led it to our house. It was surprisingly willing.

At nine that night, in the wind and the

sleet, we built a makeshift shelter in the front courtyard for the dog. It did occur to me that they say that mad dogs and English men go out in the midday sun — English men also go out in the snow and almost freeze to death to save a mad dog.

We fed the ravenous creature, gave it water, which it drank as though its life depended on it and which made me more comfortable that it didn't have rabies. Then we led it to the shelter, where it lay down on the dog bed we'd put in there and went to sleep.

This was no rabid beast; this was a scared, tired and hungry animal.

It was also huge.

The next day when we went out to the front of the house, the big black dog came bounding up to the gate of the courtyard. In the light of day it was far less frightening — still a big dog and clearly a boy, and he was wagging his tail a lot. He looked at me with his limpid dark brown eyes and I was sure I could see a bit of madness in there but mostly a longing. This was a very unhappy dog.

We went to see Monsieur Jupe again for more information. It turned out that the dog had been in the village for two weeks. It had scared the wits out of Madame Bernice down the road because it kept scratching at her back door. It had been in several gardens, scavenged for food in many dustbins. It had received absolutely no sympathy and in some cases had been kicked and hit and had things thrown at it.

So, there we were stuck with a dog everyone hated.

We checked at the town hall to see if anyone had reported him missing and left a notice on the board. We called the local SPA and they checked their database for missing dogs; nothing. Next we took him to the vet to see if he was marked.

The vet's eyes popped when we came in with the dog.

'Really?' was all he said, but in a tone that meant 'you've got to be kidding. Are you completely mad?'

'No, no, we haven't got another dog, we found him.'

'You find them all.'

'Yes, but we're not keeping him, we want to return him. We need to find his owners.'

A little while before, we'd found two spaniels lying together in the road outside Desvres on a quiet country lane. They were utterly exhausted, emaciated and pitiful creatures. We took them home, fed and watered them and took them to the vet who found their ID numbers tattooed in their ears so we were able to reunite them with their owner. The dogs, a mother and daughter, had been missing for five days and had travelled miles from home. The owner cried when he came to collect them because he was so happy. We assumed it would be the same with this dog.

The vet looked him over.

'Hmm, there is no tattoo. No markings. Nothing to identify this dog.'

We had already discussed what we would do in this scenario. Mark wanted to keep the creature. I did not.

'It is about six months old, mostly Labrador,' said the vet.

'I've always wanted a Labrador,' said Mark.

I said nothing.

'Most likely,' the vet went on, 'with this type of dog, he was being trained as a hunting dog. He probably ran away when he was let out of the cage, or he was not doing well in his training and was put in a car and thrown out somewhere.'

Hunting dogs often run away when they're allowed out. Cooped up all day and night for five to six days a week, freed at the weekend, sometimes they just run and run until they are completely lost.

'This dog,' the vet declared, 'is very wilful, I can see it in his eyes. If you keep him you will need to be strict with him, he needs a boss. By the way, I think your neighbours will start tying their old goats and cows to your front gate soon when they are too old to be of use,' he laughed.

For a week we tried hard to find out where the dog came from while he stayed in the temporary shelter. Then we introduced him to Ella Fitzgerald and Churchill and he joined them on their daily walks. He came in at night to lie in front of the fire and won the affection of 'Enry Cooper the cat by grooming him with relish. Soon he had his own bed in the dogs' room. We called him Frank Bruno, after our favourite boxer, Bruno for short, and of course he is now ours.

He is indeed very wilful, greedy and clumsy. He is also very loyal and loving, but there are certain villagers he does not like at all and growls menacingly when he sees them, perhaps remembering the hard time they gave him.

Every day starts with the same routine: feed the birds, let the cats out or in, walk the dogs.

Come rain or shine, we trundle out the gate and down the hill, up the little rue de la Chapelle and along isolated country lanes. Rue de la Chapelle consists of a few houses, a field and a tiny chapel, built by a local man as a tribute to his dearly departed wife. Big enough for two people to enter and pray in, it has stained glass windows and sculptures and looks like a miniature church that escaped from the Vatican City.

Just a couple of miles away is another chapel that is also very small, but this one is quite famous locally, known as the second Lourdes. In 1872 a local woman took ill with, it is now believed, peritonitis. In those days there was no real medical treatment for such an illness and the woman slipped into a coma. Her family held a mirror to her mouth from time to time, then the tried and tested way to see if a person was still breathing, and waited for what seemed a certain unhappy ending, as she would leave four young children motherless as well as a grieving husband. The local priest visited; he was fresh back from visiting Lourdes and brought with him a small vial of water he had acquired at the newly renowned religious site. The woman's husband, a deeply religious man, wondered if the water would bring comfort to his wife and declared that if it did he would build a chapel in honour of a benevolent and omnipotent God. The priest administered a few drops of the holy water to the woman and it is said she immediately awoke from her coma and opened her eyes. In the next few days she recovered completely and had many years of good health; she went on to have a further thirteen children with her loving husband.

As he had promised, the chapel was built. Apparently, it was only the second church ever to be dedicated to Notre Dame de Lourdes just ten years after the town had been recognized for the miraculous apparitions that were said to have appeared to local girl Bernadette Soubirous.

The little chapel, on a sharp bend on a steep hill in the middle of nowhere, remains a place of pilgrimage for locals and tourists, who are greeted with the words 'I am the Immaculate Conception' at the entrance of a white chapel with a strong Caribbean influence.

No day is ever the same on our walks, even though we often follow the same route. When there's a storm and the clouds are deep black and so low they almost touch the top of the hills that make up the Seven Valleys, the dogs run through puddles and bark at the thunder and lightning. On a crisp winter morning, they squeeze through a gap in a hedge of sloe berries to chase grouse and pheasant. In the spring, wild roses start to bud and meadow flowers appear at the sides of the road, and in the summer the tall trees offer shade to weary walkers and hot dogs.

Occasionally, we will pass a human, rarely a car, sometimes a tractor whose driver will raise a hand in greeting and acknowledgement that there is life here after all. Sometimes we will meet Thierry walking his horses back from their field to their barn. They are greedy animals and I've learned to my cost never to let them know I have an apple about me, which I do sometimes for the donkeys that live at the top of the hill. Thierry's horses will steal them from your pocket, taking half your trousers with them.

There are plenty of deer here; they stand silhouetted against the woods, motionless, watching, ready to bolt as soon as our noisy dogs get their scent. A couple of storks arrived the year before last and more have followed. Their huge nests can be seen in the trees in the distance, as big as the enormous mistletoe balls that are so much a part of the landscape here; the nests blend in seamlessly. Herons sit on fence posts, buzzards hover in the air looking for small prey, rabbits and hares run around the fields besides shrews and dormice. Bruno once disturbed a stoat, which scratched his face and scared him half to death.

If you had told me when I lived in London

that I would find one of the greatest pleasures in life was to pull on my rubber boots and wade through mud and along deserted country lanes with three excited mutts, falling in love with nature, I'd have said you were mad.

21

The birthday party

The night arrived for Jean-Claude's sixtieth birthday party. An informal affair, he had told us. 'It's *mon anniversaire* and I'm having a party in my garage.' They don't go in for embossed invitations in this part of rural France. The day before, Bernadette had stopped by to make sure we were still coming and to ask if Mark could help Jean-Claude in the morning.

'He needs to take a cupboard to the new home of my friend Madame Danton in Mark's big van,' she said, leaning in and lowering her voice as if someone close by might hear. Not really necessary since she and I were the only people in the house. 'Madame has been abandoned. Monsieur left her for a younger woman. She came home early from work at the builders' merchant and caught him having *un petit cinq-à-sept.*' French for an afternoon tryst.

She coughed discreetly and went on: 'Madame is devastated and very depressed. She has moved into a house in the next village and has no furniture so all her friends are contributing. We have an old cupboard but it is heavy and Jean-Claude, well, you know with his heart . . . '

Jean-Claude's heart is the subject of much debate in the village. He had a heart attack several years ago and tells everyone he must not do anything strenuous. He keeps vigorously to this approach to daily life, which means that even when he visits his mother-in-law Claudette just up the road, as he does several times a day, he doesn't walk; he drives the car 30 metres on the grounds that the effort would be dangerous.

Claudette and Jean-Claude garden together every day and produce vegetables for the whole family. She keeps sheep, chickens, rabbits, geese and ducks — they are not pets like my animals, they're for the pot.

Her garden backs on to ours and in the first year after we bought our French house I was determined to make our garden pretty so I sprinkled flower seeds with abandon. Each time I came to visit I could see the plants growing, and I was prepared for a colourful display to rival the Chelsea Flower Show. After a long absence due to having to work weekends in London, I came out for a week in the summer to — nothing. The young shoots that had been so promising had all but gone. Something had eaten them.

That night, as the sun went down and I sipped a gin and tonic in the garden, breathing in the scent of the countryside, I heard a rustling at the bottom of the garden.

It was one of Claudette's chickens. She had climbed a tree on Claudette's side, hopped on to a branch of a tree on my side and dropped down *Mission: Impossible*-style. She ran over to what was left of my flowerbeds and started scrabbling around in the dirt.

We shooed her off and put her back over the fence. She did the same thing the next night. We tried cutting the branches but the hen simply found another way in; she was the Rambo of the chicken world.

'Let's take her back to Claudette,' I said to Mark. 'Perhaps she'll know how to stop her, clip her wings or something like that.'

Mark caught the bird and we wandered into Claudette's courtyard. The door is only closed when she goes to bed.

I explained that the chicken kept coming into the garden and eating my flowers and asked if it was possible to do something to keep her out.

'Sure,' said Claudette and rung the bird's neck on the doorstep.

'It's a bit earlier than I planned but she will do for Sunday,' she said smiling sweetly.

240

Whenever any of her animals come into our garden now, we keep quiet.

Claudette wasn't going to Jean-Claude's party that night; she goes to bed at precisely 7 p.m. and has done for many years. She rises at 5.30, as she has every morning since she married in 1950 and would make her husband's breakfast before he went off to work as a farmer.

We had been told the party would start at 7.30 p.m. We took no notice of this, though, having been caught out before. When French people say a time you should visit, they don't mean it — I don't understand why they don't just say the time they really want you there in the first place. Once we were invited for dinner at a French neighbours' house.

'Come at 7 p.m.,' they said. So we did. We were new to it then and didn't know any better.

We arrived precisely on time. Our hostess opened the door with a quizzical look. A look that said, 'Who could this possibly be? I am not expecting anyone at 7 p.m.' When she saw us standing there she was most taken aback.

'Bonsoir,' I said, trying to cover the awkward moment that could not be avoided since I heard her husband call, 'Who is it, cherie?'

'Have we got the wrong night?'

241

It turns out you must always be at least ten to fifteen minutes later than asked. I once asked Jean-Claude and Bernadette to drinks with some other neighbours and they turned up two hours after the time I told them and thought that was fine!

For Jean-Claude's birthday party we thought we had it nailed. We would go at 8 p.m.

We wandered down the hill with a bottle of whisky for the birthday boy and heard loud music coming from the town hall.

'Are you sure it's in the garage?' I said to Mark as another couple of neighbours in front of us turned into the drive of the Mairie, the town hall, clutching gifts.

Jean-Claude lives close to the Mairie so, though we were tempted to go with the flow, we thought we'd better make sure. We used the pedestrian crossing that the mayor had commissioned — for a village of 142 people through which several cars a day pass — and immediately saw Jean-Claude's garage swing door was up — a good sign. Unbelievably, almost all of the guests were there already. Sometimes I realize that it doesn't matter how long I have been here, how much I think I have learned, I am never going to get it right.

Jean-Claude's garage contains the central

heating boiler system for his house and Bernadette's car, but for festive occasions, of which there are several a year, the car is removed and tables and chairs are laid out. It is the perfect party parlour, albeit with a bit of a hiss from the boiler. As with all get-togethers in France, one must kiss before one does anything else. Two kisses, starting on the left in our village. It takes a while to kiss thirty people and Bernadette had a Kir petulant waiting for me.

'There's a wedding on at the Mairie tonight,' she said. 'But I bet we keep going longer than they do.' I could tell we were in for a long night.

At the bar that had been set up in the garage, made from wooden pallets by our Belgian neighbours, there was a serious discussion going on about how to open the barrel of Belgian beer they had brought with them. It was one of those metal canisters that goes into a beer dispenser but unfortunately, the fittings for the French machine did not fit the Belgian cask. This was a serious issue. When one brings a gift for all to enjoy, it must be enjoyed by all — it's an unspoken law.

'We could maybe make an adaptor,' suggested Petit-Frère hopefully. He is called that by everyone in the village and I suspect it's not just me who doesn't know his real name. He has nine older brothers and sisters (he is forty-nine) and so has always been called Petit-Frère (little brother).

After a bit of fumbling with some tube, that idea was dismissed.

Aha, said everyone, the day is saved, when a young man said that he had a fitting at home that would work. He dashed to his car and drove off at speed.

'Where does he live?' I asked.

'About thirty minutes' drive away,' came the answer.

While he was gone, everyone drank bottled and canned beer. It was a hot, humid night, and the beer was laced with Picon, which creates a sort of beer cocktail. I'm not a beer drinker but it was very fruity and refreshing on a hot night, and also very strong.

Of course, we could not start the barbecue until the return of the man with the machine fitting, though by now it was 10 p.m. When he finally arrived, everyone breathed a sigh of relief while a couple of men fidgeted about with the part to see if they could mend the beer machine. The sausages were put on, and local spicy merguez and other types sizzled deliciously under a half moon with a sky that was brimming with stars. The table heaved with salads, breads, olives and other delicious food.

Bernadette, ever the perfect hostess, encouraged us to eat our fill . . . the night was young yet!

Music and dancing followed dinner. The garage door was closed, the tables cleared, the beer machine got a cheer when finally it was used. One man looked thoroughly miserable throughout, though. Paul is a university professor, has written several books and is a French academic of the old school. He loves to talk in long, flowing, flowery sentences, frankly boring everyone to bits. He is in his late fifties and looks rather worse for wear thanks to his fondness for home-made crème de menthe. Not something I recommend, by the way: drink a whole glass and you're likely to wake up on the floor the next day with no memory after the first sip (but if you have a cold it will be cured).

Last Christmas Paul stunned everyone by managing to persuade coquettish Sylvie from the next village to go out with him. Twenty years younger, incredibly pretty in a sultry French way, she can have her pick of beaux and has a reputation for being somewhat choosy.

Quite what she saw in Paul with his scruffy, smelly suits, ancient falling-down house and his habit of talking for hours on end is beyond everyone.

But love is strange.

And in this case it is stranger than usual.

Several weeks into their budding relationship, Paul found a baby chicken in his garden. For Paul it was a *coup de foudre*. During the week Sylvie works away from home as an advertising executive in Paris and Paul was alone as usual. He took the chicken in, bought it food and accoutrements and called it Cherie.

When I say he took the chicken in, I mean in the house, to live with him.

When Sylvie came back at the weekend, she went to visit Paul and was charmed by his attachment to the little bird. The pair of them spent the weekend cooing over it.

Paul's affection for Cherie grew. He took her everywhere with him. We all looked out for his car to pass so we could spot Cherie sitting on his shoulder like the ugliest parrot that ever lived. Cherie continued to live in the house, running around freely (and doing what chickens do) and sleeping in a box on top of Paul's bed.

Sylvie started to resent Cherie, and really, who can blame her? It all came to a head when Sylvie decided enough was enough when Paul suggested Cherie might like to sleep on the pillow instead of in a box.

'It's me or Cherie,' Sylvie said to Paul.

Soppy he may be, stupid he is not.

Cherie was adopted by a local farmer after he promised to cherish her and Paul went home to Sylvie who wiped away his tears. Alas, by the time of Jean-Claude's party, Sylvie had recently dumped Paul; it seems she had met a younger professor with a smart car and a clean suit who didn't sulk about a lost chicken love.

Mark and I staggered home from the party in the early hours of the morning.

As we passed the town hall, the music was still playing loudly but when we looked through the windows to see what was going on, there were just four men playing cards round a small table and one man dancing on his own in the middle of the *salle des fêtes*, dressed as a cowboy with a long leather coat over the top, *Matrix*-style. In this heat! Typically French, neither party wanted to be the first to give in.

We opened the door to our little house, fell up the stairs and into a deep sleep where I dreamed that I gave birth to a baby made of gingerbread and woke up vowing never to drink Picon beer again.

The next day was my own birthday. Money was as usual quite tight and we were making sure we stretched our savings as much as possible, so we decided that for my birthday I would get a cup of tea in bed, which was fine with me since I am always the one who gets up to let the dogs and cats out and feed the birds. However, I got a present that day I had never expected.

A pathetic little black kitten turned up at the back door. He was starving, bald in places and had an awful eye disease that was so bad his inner eyelids covered his eyes permanently — they were horribly red and swollen. He had fleas, cat flu and worms. He was feral and vicious: when I tried to pick him up to take him to the vets he bit me so hard his sharp little teeth went right through my fingernail, leaving me with an infection. It was my fault, as the poor thing was in pain and terrified and he could hardly see.

Though I really did not want another animal, I couldn't just let the poor creature die and I could tell he was suffering. For a week I put food out for him at the back door. He made himself a bed on top of a bale of hay in the garden and ate the food. It got so I could pick him up safely and pop him in a cat crate and I took him to my lovely vet.

'How many cats is this now?' he asked.

'Well, if I keep this one it will be number six,' I told him.

'You have to stop this. I've seen it before with you expats. You have one cat, then two, then six and then twenty-six. You will be my best customer, but it isn't good for you and not for your cats. Promise you will try to stop.'

I said I would try. I don't want this to keep happening, I travel a lot and Mark, my friends and family have to look after the zoo when I'm not there. But I couldn't leave a sick, starving creature to just fade away like that.

'It is nature,' said my sensible vet, and of course I know he is right but . . .

I named the kitten Hank Marvin on account of the fact that he was starvin'. I regret to tell you that everyone else calls him Skank Marvin on account of the fact that he is extremely skanky. His hair has never fully grown back, his eye infection has left him blind in one eye and he will never be a big cat, always a runt, but a happy runt.

The same week Hank Marvin turned up, another one of my ducks had babies. That is, her eggs hatched. Unfortunately, this first-time mother duck had led her five ducklings into a pond and they couldn't get out. I found one of them frantically paddling, the other four had drowned and the mum was nowhere to be seen. I brought the plucky little survivor into the house, rubbed it dry and put it under a red lamp to warm up. Lucky, as I called it, lived in a trolley (don't ask) at the side of my desk for three weeks. I am not sure what my vet would have made of this story. With no competent mum to care for this duckling, he would likely have just perished in the garden and he needed time to grow stronger before he joined the rest. For quite a while after he was rehabilitated into the duck pen he followed me around as if he was tied by string to my shoes.

Despite my best intentions, I appear to have turned into an expat Crazy Cat Lady. An expat Crazy Dog Lady. An expat Crazy Chicken and Duck Lady.

22

The land of milk and honey

It became clear that having a big garden in the middle of the countryside in France was not going to be a walk in the park.

Before we lived permanently in the old farmhouse, every visit had been a battle to gain control of the house and the garden. An acre of land might not sound like much but when you're used to a space that is just about big enough to walk round your parked car, it's a daunting prospect.

We couldn't afford to pay someone to cut the grass and keep it neat, so we just had to roll up our sleeves and get on with it. In my naïvety I was sure that once we lived there full time, the garden would somehow become more manageable. I was wrong.

We decided to indulge in a ride-on mower to help make cutting an acre of grass easier and more fun. Not just for us, as it turned out.

One sunny summer afternoon Mark was riding leisurely round the garden when what we assumed was one of our neighbours suddenly appeared from nowhere on his own ride-on mower. We'd never seen him before and he didn't introduce himself.

He drove on to the grass and started racing my totally bemused husband. Up and down they went uttering not a word to each other. It was hardly Le Mans but they were both in it to win it.

As they 'raced' down to the last lap of the lawn with all the speed of a pair of determined but geriatric snails, the neighbour pulled away, raised a hand and disappeared back out of the gate.

As we heard him riding off into the distance, we stood for a moment in quiet contemplation.

'Did that just happen?' said Mark.

'Yes. You just had possibly the slowest race in the world. I think I might phone the Guinness Book of World Records.'

'Who was it?'

'I don't know.'

'Look at the grass.'

'Yes, it looks like dyslexic aliens have visited and made quite possibly the worst crop circles in history.'

'At least it's done.'

'Let's cut the hedge — he might come back.'

Actually, we have never seen him again;

perhaps he wasn't a neighbour after all and the mower was his means of getting about. It is possible.

I was once in the car park of the supermarket in Fruges when a tractor pulled up next to my car and a family of four disembarked from the cab and went in to do their shopping. Returning to their tractor, they put their goods in the bucket, hopped back into the cabin and drove off.

We came to discover that neighbours simply walking or driving into our garden would be a common occurrence.

Our land was actually two small fields separated by a ragged hawthorn hedge, with more fields at the bottom. To make grass cutting easier we decided to remove the hedge with or without the random stranger on his ride-on mower. It was not a task to be relished. We approached with caution, as the hedge was old and prickly and its roots were deep. Three hours later we had hardly made a dent in it. Jean-Claude came wandering in; he had most likely been watching the idiot English people from over the fence and, exasperated by our pitiful efforts, came to offer a hand.

'My tractor will make short work of that. I will go and get it,' he announced and walked back out. Life in the country is very much give and take. If Jean-Claude has a loose tile on the roof he will call on Mark whom he calls *Le Singe* (the monkey). Mark has no fear of heights or climbing to the top of a roof via a wobbly ladder.

Jean-Claude returned shortly afterwards driving his ancient held-together-with-plasters Massey Ferguson. He instructed us to tie a rope around a bush and then to the back of the tractor. He drove forward and, 'PLOP', out came the bushes as one by one we made our way up the garden. The bushes weren't the only thing that came out, though. The gaping holes revealed a wealth of rubbish, old roof tiles, plastic boxes and even a rusty old motorbike. Someone had been using the garden as a rubbish dump and had dug great holes either side of the bushes to bury unwanted items. Over the years nature had covered the scrap heap with grass so we'd never noticed that there was anything under there. It felt that everything we did to try to improve the house simply led to more work and more problems.

Still, by the end of the afternoon the hedge was gone and we celebrated with a bottle of red wine.

The three of us sat on the terrace (a square of concrete at the back of the kitchen) in friendly contemplation of the mess we'd made.

Me: 'Were you born here, Jean-Claude?'

'Non. I am a stranger here.'

'A stranger?'

'Yes, I was born five kilometres away.'

'That makes you a stranger?'

'Yes, in this village you are a stranger unless you are born here. My wife was born here, so she is not a stranger.'

It was pretty obvious we would have our work cut out to become part of this community.

'How many people are there in the village?' I asked.

'One hundred and forty-two humans and a thousand cows,' laughed Jean-Claude. 'Do you know the story of Monsieur Martin and his cows? Non? Well, he keeps his cows in that field at the top of the hill — you must have seen them come charging down when he calls them for dinner? It's so steep, once they get going they cannot stop until they reach the level at the bottom. Well, anyway, one day he went to call the cows and some of them were gone. They had got out into the road and wandered off.'

He stopped to take a big slurp of his wine.

'He went to look for them and found some of them staggering around at the bottom of the village. He said they looked drunk and very unwell. He was very worried and went to get his friends to help him find the other cows.'

More wine; thirsty work this storytelling.

'They called and looked and eventually found the rest of the cows in the garden of an empty house and they were all acting very strangely. They were falling over and just lying there looking happily into space. Monsieur Martin got his cows back to the field where they just lay down. He thought they might have been poisoned so he called the gendarmes. They went to the empty house to look around and discovered the entire garden was covered in marijuana plants. Someone had been growing them there and the cows had eaten some. They were sky high.'

He chortled away to himself, finished his wine and ambled off with a wink.

It took us several weeks to clear the garden of the rubbish, which enabled us to discover the pleasure of visiting a *déchetterie* — a municipal rubbish dump.

We were dreading a trip to dispose of the rubbish we'd dug up, which by now also included a large fridge. In London we'd had to provide evidence of where we lived, pay to dispose of certain pieces, fill in forms and all sorts of administration. With its reputation for bureaucracy we figured the French requirements were going to be really dreadful. We loaded the rubbish on to the trailer and headed to Beaurainville and our nearest rubbish tip.

We drove in, were waved to pull over and one of the workmen came over. We were ready: we had utility bills, passports and all sorts. He looked in the trailer and started to throw the rubbish into a skip. We leaped to help him. And that was that. The most friendly, helpful people work at that rubbish dump and over the years we've come to know them well — we once estimated we may have cleared more than 20 tonnes of rubbish from the house and garden.

You might think I am exaggerating but I assure you I am not. Originally a barn, the house had dirt floors in several rooms. Even though it had passed through the hands of several families since cows were the main proprietors, the work was what you might call ongoing when we bought the house. In fact, it still is and probably always will be. That is the nature of homes in the country.

We had been able to find out some of the history of the house from Jean-Claude. It was once the village telephone exchange and there is still an ancient 'téléphone' sign in one of the rooms. In the 1950s and 1960s people from the village would come here to use the phone. They could also get a cup of coffee, a beer or a glass of wine while they waited for their connection. To be perfectly honest, there are times when I could happily pour myself a glass of wine while I'm working because the internet speed is so slow; there are days when I could get a message to my friend in the next village more quickly if I just drove there.

There used to be hundreds of houses in this area that acted as telephone exchanges; some had a TV where villagers could congregate to watch, some were small shops and bars. To this day there are still homes where you can go to buy a drink and many of the bars are also shops where you can buy all manner of items you'd never expect, such as children's sweets in the shape of toilets. I'm not kidding, I've actually bought them. (How can you resist a miniature toilet with a lolly that you dip in the bowl, which is filled with sherbert?)

In the little village of Hesmond is a 'pub' that is the home of a local woman called Adeline. She is quite elderly and has run a bar for decades. You simply go up to her front door. If it's warm you can enjoy your beer or coffee in the garden outside, and if it's cold you can sit at the table in her front room. It's very popular with the local farmers who stop in on their way to and from work.

One day Jean-Claude came to our door, huffing and puffing as usual.

'Can I borrow Mark, just for a couple of minutes?'

This is how it always starts. Sometimes it is a couple of minutes, sometimes it is for considerably longer. It is the way of the countryside here. Neighbours help each other out and Jean-Claude repays us in many ways for utilizing Mark's relative youth and strength. A trailer load of dried wood, a tray of plums, or even a goose or two. Yes, once I made the mistake of telling Jean-Claude that I thought a goose would be fun to have in the garden. Later that day Mark and I were invited down to his house and into the back garden where he keeps his pigeons, rabbits, chickens, ducks and geese. Jean-Claude produced a basket and then, with Mark's aid, attempted to catch a male and a female goose. After much cursing and falling over I was presented with a basket containing two very angry hissing geese.

They are remarkably ungrateful birds, but I've grown fond of them, and they make excellent guards.

Anyway, on this occasion Mark's input was all over quite quickly, but the memory of this task will live with us forever.

'My tractor won't start,' said Jean-Claude.

This is nothing new, lately it never starts. Somehow Jean-Claude always manages to get it out of the garage where it lives at the top of the hill in his mother-in-law's garden. Once he gets it out on to the steep road, he bump starts it on the way down the hill and by the time it gets to the bottom it has, so far, always managed to fire into life.

This time, however, it had a trailer on the back and Jean-Claude couldn't move it on his own.

Mark went with him up the hill. Jean-Claude clambered up into the tractor 'to turn the wheel the right way' and called to Mark to push. Mark pushed. He is a big, heavy bloke and very strong. Nothing happened.

'Push!' yelled Jean-Claude. Mark gritted his teeth, jammed his shoulder against the trailer and heaved as if his life depended on it. Nothing happened.

'We can do it,' called Jean-Claude from his seat in the tractor, blissfully unaware of the division of labour.

'Un, deux, trois!' he shouted and Mark pushed one more time and to his utter amazement the tractor and trailer lurched forward and on to the hill. Oh the joy, the pride, the belief in his manly power. Until he looked down and saw Claudette standing there brushing the dust off her pinafore.

'That was heavy, wasn't it?' she said without a modicum of irony.

Claudette has been widowed for many years and now lives alone in the biggest house in the village. Her brother lived with her for a short while before sadly passing away. He was old and disabled and Claudette cared for him and took him for a daily walk round the village in his wheelchair. She is as slight as a sparrow, and her brother was rather larger and heavier. He had been a farmer, short and sturdy, slinging sacks of grain that weighed 45 kilos or more over his shoulder 'like a lady with a handbag', he said. But the years of heavy lifting took their toll and, single, he moved into his sister's house. At eighty years old he could not walk but was confined to a rather sturdy wheelchair. Despite this she pushed him up and down the hills of the village and rejected all offers of help.

'Non, non. It's good exercise,' she told me when, concerned for both her and her brother, I offered to help. It's a steep hill with a road at the bottom, and I had visions of her tripping, letting go and the wheelchair careering down and into an oncoming tractor. When she wasn't pushing her brother, she'd usually have a basket of eggs, fruit or vegetables to give to a neighbour.

While everyone in the village grows something in the garden or keeps animals of various sorts, there are also quite a few artisans, who choose to produce food or goods the traditional way — organic, of course. It's a time-consuming business but these people are passionate about the land and maintaining traditions of the past as a way to protect the future.

In the tiny village of Hesmond, you'd be forgiven for thinking the residents had dropped down dead. As you drive along the little roads that lead there you may pass a tractor or two, a few cars or a curious cow with its head poking over the top of a hedge. This *ville tranquille*, as it is known, is rarely lively. Unless, that is, it is one of the days when Valérie Magniez, also known locally as 'the goat lady', bakes bread. Then you will find to your astonishment that the single main road of the village is packed full of cars and bikes as locals and tourists alike head for her farm. They are here to buy the organic country bread that goes so perfectly with the fresh goats' cheese that the goat lady makes daily. Rumour has it that she uses a four-hundred-year-old live yeast mix, although when I asked she would neither confirm nor deny it.

Valérie's goats outnumber the residents by

a long shot. She talks to them, milks them — the goats that is, not the people — except for the very large billy goat known as l'Amoureux, and makes the most amazing cheese by hand, every day of the week, with love. Eaten fresh, it is a little sour, creamy and seductive, and everyone goes back for more.

At the counter she will offer to sprinkle fresh herbs as she wraps up the little cheeses and she will encourage you to go to meet her goats in their bespoke barn, usually accompanied by the farmyard cat and often kittens that run about playing with stones and generally getting in everyone's way.

The shop is only open a few hours a week, on days when Valérie fires up her big old wood oven and the smoke rises above the roof of the Gothic-looking wooden home that she and her husband built. On those occasions, this normally placid little village comes to life.

A little way down the road in the village of Offin, François Delepierre grows vegetables. Not just any old vegetables either. He and his mother grow heirloom produce in a field at the back of their house. In these lush valleys the soil is rich and nourishing. Drive down the somewhat misleadingly named Grande Rue where the Delepierre farm is located and, if you blink, you'll miss the sign for Aux Légumes d'Antan (*d'antan* means 'of yesteryear'). And that would be a great loss for you because this little place is a treasure trove of fabulous vegetables and fruit, sold in the ancient shed that serves as a shop and dished up at lunchtime in the front room of their house, which functions as a restaurant on Sundays only. It is like having dinner with friends: unpretentious, modest, hearty and wholesome, and, like Valérie's goats' cheese, made with passion.

Wash it down with local beer or cider, or even sparkling wine made with redcurrants, strawberries or raspberries by Hubert Delobel in the village of Loisin, made to a recipe his grandmother used, now an award-winning, wonderfully delicious drink, perfect for festive occasions.

Here in the countryside, people may not be wealthy or live in swish posh houses, but in so many ways the good life is all around if you take the time to find it.

23

Home is where the heart is

France is famous for its second-hand markets, *brocantes*, *marchés aux puces*, *braderies* and *vide-greniers* — flea markets are known by several names and they are held in all regions. They take place throughout the year, mostly on weekends, the majority of them from March to October when better weather means stalls can be laid out in the streets of towns and villages with less chance of getting drenched. Going to a flea market is a way of life in France; it isn't just about finding a bargain, though this is a nation of recyclers. For the French it's a great way to meet with friends and socialize. For visitors it's a chance to get under the skin of a place, to experience the national culture.

There is almost always a 'buffet' of some sort, often involving a frites wagon, and delights such as local sausages, pancakes or a hog roast. Some flea markets are specialists where vendors sell only high-quality antiques, stamps, military memorabilia or clothes. Other markets are full of local people who empty out their lofts and cellars, pile up their odds and ends on a blanket on the ground or sell off unwanted farm machinery. You'll usually find stalls specializing in old linen, china, religious relics, ex-hotel tableware, and of course there is a lot of junk. I'm always amazed by the number of people who sell way-past-their-prime collections: there is always a motley assortment of jam jars, broken cups, gas pipes, light fittings, rusty garden implements and even old bottle corks. It's a mystery to me who buys this stuff but I suppose someone must or they wouldn't be on show.

I've rarely been to a bad flea market. There's always something new to discover, if not on the stalls, then on the journey, which you can be sure will involve a road diversion of some sort, guaranteed to create chaos on the way in as well as out.

Saint-Valery-sur-Somme on the edge of the Somme Estuary is where you will find arguably one of the most beautiful bays in the world. It's a town with a lively atmosphere and some grand villas that once lured writers from Victor Hugo to Collette, Anatole France and Jules Verne, all inspired by the scenery to stay awhile and write. As well as the stunning views, the other big draw here is the harbour, which is lined with restaurants whose tables sprawl on to the pavement, filled with diners indulging in fresh, locally caught fish.

The town has several claims to fame, not least the fact that Joan of Arc was held in a château here (it has sadly long gone) prior to being taken to Rouen and her horrible demise. There is a statue dedicated to her on the edge of the bay in Place Jeanne d'Arc with a lovely little walkway where boules is played and children scan the inlet for basking seals. It is largely the French who visit this family friendly holiday haven and it's a well-kept secret. I first went there with my dad, and if you ever worry about how bad your French is, you needn't, there's always someone worse. There was a poster in the town advertising something to do with Jeanne d'Arc or, as my dad pronounced it, 'Jenny Dark'.

You can take a boat ride around the horseshoe-shaped bay and watch fishermen bringing in their haul of the day on their bright little fishing boats. At the Chemin de Fer railway station, from late spring to the end of summer eager passengers hop on board a steam train and ride round the bay through picturesque countryside, stopping off at the bigger towns like Le Crotoy, across the bay.

This is where hundreds of sellers meet

once a year to sell antiques and all manner of junk. It never ceases to amaze me that parking is so easy in most of northern France and usually free. Aiming to find a café where we could start the day off properly with a steaming cup of strong coffee and a pain au chocolat, we wandered along streets full of little cottages from which the local fishermen were selling fresh seafood. An old salty seadog type, wearing his sou'wester and boots, was carrying a tray of shrimp he had just caught and saw me admiring them.

'Come back in five minutes when they're cooked,' he told me. How could I resist?

When I returned, he had set up a table on the pavement under his front window and did a roaring trade selling the still-warm shrimp; they were so fresh and sweet. At the brocante that ran along the seafront, about three hundred stalls in all, the whole place was buzzing as the early morning mist cleared, the sky turned a deep blue and the warm sun made it a very pleasant occasion indeed. At least until I managed to tread in dog poo.

'I'm not going anywhere with you unless you clean it off,' said Mark.

So I found a bit of grass and was busy rubbing the offending foot.

A man standing close by was watching me, cursing.

'Anglaise?' he asked, and then told me that I was lucky it was my left foot, chuckling to himself.

'If it was your right foot, not so lucky,' he chortled.

The old man wasn't kidding. Treading in dog poo with your left foot is considered fortunate in France. I even found an online shop trying to 'crapitalize' on this weird superstition by selling 'Lucky dog shit from Paris', though apparently it wasn't a best-seller.

Further round the coast, a very special festival takes place in the little fishing village of Audresselles, also in spring. It is tucked away off the main A16 autoroute that leads to the south, on the glorious D940 coastal road, which starts at Calais and runs along an undulating, green and sometimes dramatic shoreline.

Along this twisting, winding road, which meanders through picturesque villages and clifftop towns facing the White Cliffs of Dover, you will find a rather hidden part of France. It is known as the Côte d'Opale (Opal Coast) and runs for 120 km from Dunkerque on the edge of the border with Belgium to Berck-sur-Mer, 20 km from Le Crotoy. The name Opal Coast originated from the many nineteenth-century painters who flocked here to capture the area's natural beauty and the light's opal-like qualities. The great British painter J. M. W. Turner loved this region and his painting of Calais pier on a stormy day hangs in the National Gallery in London. Visiting the little hamlets on this route will take you back in time to a more gentle age when the families of fishermen would be waiting on the beach to help take in the day's catch and sell it to the public from their homes — a practice that continues to this day all around this stretch of the coastline.

Indeed, nothing much seems to have changed in the village of Audresselles in several decades. Fish are caught by hand from *flobards*, the traditional flat-bottomed boats that have been used since time immemorial in this area. Tractors pull the boats up on to the sandy beaches and the bounty is sold direct from the homes of the locals. Madame Baillet sells the fish from the garage of her house at rue Gustave Danquin, brought in fresh each day by her sons Stéphane and François. She tells customers how proud she is to be a part of this tradition, and is typical of the people that live and work here.

The annual Fête du Crabe is held in honour, of course, of the crab, which is plentiful in these parts. Fishermen and women wade out into rock pools via a Jurassic-looking natural breakwater formed of immense boulders. Carrying crates to put their catch in, they return to the village with fresh shellfish to sell to visitors, who arrive here for a fabulous lunch and to enjoy the fête.

Bands play, there is bagpipe music, majorettes and sea shanties. Local folk-dancing group Les Bretons de Dunkerque perform on stage to huge applause and I always think how warm they must be in their heavy, dark costumes, the gold brocade glinting as they whirl around.

There is a lot to enjoy but it's the crab that hogs the limelight. Served with freshly baked bread, it is simple but delicious.

Take time to explore this beautiful coastline and you'll discover ancient forts and Second World War bunkers and museums. Climb the Colonne de la Grande Armée in Wimille, near Boulogne — a fifty-metre tower erected in honour of Napoleon on the spot where he issued the first Légion d'honneur medals on 16 August 1804, and where almost two thousand years earlier Julius Caesar planned his invasion of Britain. The country-side here is delightful, a mosaic of colours against the backdrop of the English Channel.

Tiny towns with artisan boulangeries and charcuteries tempt you to stop and discover the local specialities and stay to enjoy the peace and tranquillity.

On the last Sunday in August the town of Le Touquet Paris-Plage holds its annual flea market. We sat at the little Café Le Copo listening to the band from neighbouring resort Berck-sur-Mer. Me, Mark and our friend Gary.

This trendy seaside resort in northern France is the secret 'get away from it all' destination of Parisians as well as Brits in the know. At less than an hour's drive from Calais it offers the chance for a perfect break all year round, with its long golden sandy beaches and pretty Belle Epoque villas, gourmet shops, fabulous restaurants, great golf courses, horse riding, tennis — I could go on and on. For a small seaside resort, Le Touquet packs a big punch.

I don't need any excuses to visit Le Touquet, I adore its retro style — from the listed historic covered market place to the glorious early twentieth-century villas, the town hall and hotels. The whole town is like one great homage to art deco and hints at its hedonistic past as the playground of choice for the wealthy and famous in the first half of the twentieth century. Noël Coward, Marlene

Dietrich, P. G. Wodehouse, Winston Churchill — they all loved this little town — much for the same reason I love it today. It has class.

So, there we were, the band playing 'Peter Gunn' (think *Blues Brothers*). It was overcast, the first time in weeks after a good long summer, but everyone was smiling and happy.

Mamans stopped with babies in pushchairs to listen to the band, two little girls with braided hair were dancing in the pedestrianized road, and oldies were tapping their feet, arms crossed. Gary pointed out that the cool dude playing the tuba was only using one hand and indeed he was — it was that sort of band.

We ordered three *grands crèmes*. I always hope to have American-style big cups of coffee but, as often happens, it was a miniature strong espresso, in a big cup. At least there was an entire day for my eyes to be wide open after this hit.

An old lady, tiny and crooked, ambled past with a basket and a baguette, waiters wandered in and out of the tables and chairs that spilled out of Le Copo on to the pavement. Fashionable Parisians, tanned from a month at their impossibly posh and stylish second homes in the north, sat and enjoyed the last of the summer before La

Rentrée (the return to normal ... work, Paris), the men wearing leather hats, pink jumpers tied jauntily round their shoulders, the ladies wearing Hermes scarves and carrying chic shopping bags.

'Sometimes,' said Gary, 'living in northern France is like living in Trumpton.'

I know what he meant. Trumpton is an imaginary town that featured in a children's programme in the UK, where the town hall clock told the time 'steadily, sensibly; never too quickly, never too slowly' — the perfect town, the one that fired children's imaginations.

A man walked by; he had a rolled-up carpet tucked under one arm and balanced on top of the plaster of Paris that covered his other arm. We were reminded why we were there and set off to look for something unique with a bit of history.

Since this town is such an art deco utopia I hoped to find something appropriate and I wasn't disappointed as, almost immediately I found an immaculate 1930s toaster and then a silver art deco desk calendar — in perfect condition and just a few euros each.

We browsed and bargained and bought until lunchtime and decided on a whim to go to the café Le Fireman. Just off the main high street, this place is not touristy — it's authentic and very friendly. The waiters wear long red aprons, and call out orders to the bar staff while balancing their trays precariously and with style. It seemed we were not the only ones looking for the real deal, as the place was buzzing with glamorous blondes and tanned gents quaffing pre-lunch apéritifs.

When a grandad came into the bar with his young grandson, the waiter bent down to the four-year-old to take the order for his juice and Grandad's beer as if he was the most important customer in the place. The old man and the young child sat on the long retro banquette and had an animated conversation, separated by seventy years but not noticing.

In came a perfectly coiffed and manicured woman of a certain age. The waiter kissed her on both cheeks, saying, 'Ah, Anita . . . ma cherie'; the barman prepared a Kir royale without a word passing between him, the waiter and the elegant Anita. I couldn't help thinking how much I longed to be French in that effortless, sophisticated, elegant way that French women have.

I wandered up to the bar and one of the waiters said, 'Ah, I know you: The Good Life France. I know your website.' It was one of the most surreal moments. 'I am Franck,' he said, 'from the tourist office. I am just helping my friend Grègoire who owns Le Fireman as he's so busy today.' We kissed on the cheek, and just like that, I felt as though my dream had come true.

Life's not always about great monuments, it's about great moments — and feeling accepted by the place you've adopted as your new home. It was as if France had wrapped her arms around me and given me a hug of welcome.

24

The end or, rather, the beginning

There is a saying in this part of France that goes: *Les gens du nord ont le soleil dans le coeur.* The people in the north have the sun in their hearts. They need to, as it actually does rain rather often here. But it's true: they are a very friendly lot, generous in spirit and welcoming. In fact, of all the places I've been to, I have never met a more hospitable or affable bunch of people, and the weather doesn't get them down.

I've stood at the top of beautiful hilltop villages in Provence and dreamed of living there, knowing that the sun would come out to play most days. I've fallen in love with Burgundy and Champagne, with the Loire Valley and Honfleur, with Paris and Marseille. I've never seen so many awesome restaurants as there are in Lyon; Bordeaux left me sighing when I departed.

But, wherever I go, I'm always happy to return to the north of France despite the lack of predictable sunshine.

I've been made welcome by the people who

live here and it feels like home. When the elderly brother of a neighbour was introduced to me he narrowed his eyes. 'Are you from the south?' he said. 'You don't sound local.'

'No,' I replied, thrilled to bits that he thought my French that good. 'I'm English.'

'English,' he said, 'not French.' He paused and concluded philosophically, 'Ah well, nobody is perfect.'

Whenever I come back from my travels, I push open the gate that squeaks like a frightened mouse and sets the dogs in the village off barking. My cats come bounding into the garden from sheds and outbuildings, from hedges and barns. My dogs woof a noisy welcome; Ella Fitzgerald wags her tail so much it's like the rotors of a helicopter. The geese start honking, the chickens cluck and the ducks quack. Without fail, that last sound takes me right back to that very first day when, pulling up outside this old house on a cold, wet, grey and depressingly dismal day in February about ten years ago, the sun came out and I heard the sound of fate . . . and the start of a new life beckoned.

How to be a successful expat in France

Thirty tips to living the good life in France based on real life, and a tongue-in-cheek list to help would-be expats settle and fit in quickly.

1. Absinthe makes the mind go wander
Beware the friend who offers a glass of absinthe — water it down, drink it slow or you will wake up not knowing who you are or where you are. The French call absinthe *la fée verte*, which literally means 'the green fairy' — drink too much of it and you are likely to see green fairies in the bottom of the toilet bowl.

2. There's something about Mairie
Always make friends with the mayor and his or her staff. The mayor can be helpful or not, but it is best to make sure. Some expats swear by giving the mayor a bottle of whisky when they move to their new home, but some French people view such currying favour as potentially suspicious and think you will want

something from them. A French friend tells me you should never smile too much at the mayor (or at someone in an interview or meeting) because it's almost certain they will suspect you have something to hide behind that grin.

3. A kiss is just a kiss

Kiss, don't hug. On the whole, the French are not huggers and will be horrified if you throw your arms around them and pull them close against you — kissing them on the face up to four times is fine, though. It's a mystery to foreigners how many times to kiss, and on what side to start. Actually, even French people get confused because in some regions you kiss once, others twice, three times, even four times. It also depends on who you're kissing. For instance, you shouldn't kiss your boss — unless he or she initiates the process. Elderly relatives generally get more kisses; men kiss if they are good friends or related. If you're not sure, follow the lead of the French person you're with. Two kisses is a safe bet, starting on the right!

4. Being late is fashionable

Never turn up to a party or dinner on time. You will find your host half dressed and irritated. Be at least fifteen minutes late and don't apologize. Quite why French people don't make the invite for the time they actually want you to arrive is not yet known.

5. Don't wine
Never take a bottle of wine to a dinner party. Take flowers or chocolates. Some French people think if you take wine you are indicating that they don't know how to choose the right wine for their guests.

6. I'm not piscine about
In French swimming pools, men are not allowed to wear swimming shorts. Instead, by law they must wear tight-fitting, clinging triangles of material. You had better pack your budgie smugglers if you want to go swimming here.

Apparently, it's all about hygiene.

Yes, you read that right.

You have to wear teeny weeny body-hugging Speedo-style trunks to the pool in France because it's more hygienic. 'Ladies' knickers', my neighbour calls them, or, to give them their proper French name, *slip de bain* or *tin boxer*.

According to the powers that be, you might wear your baggy swim shorts as normal shorts, and if you do they may pick up dust and dirt and suchlike. But, the clever and all powerful ones cunningly surmise, no man is going to wander around the dusty streets wearing his tiny, barely modesty-covering nylon horror pants, is he? So, when he puts them on to enter the pristine waters of a public pool, they will be clean. I can only assume they have not visited the beaches of the south of France where barely there pants are much in evidence both off and on the beaches. I can sort of understand the hygiene aspects but we all know that little kids wee in the pool, so it's really rather a moot point to worry about a bit of dust on a pair of trunks.

In fact, this is a law harking back to 1903 when longer swimming shorts were banned by the government and, despite this rather tricky subject being raised numerous times in parliament for an update, so far it's a firm 'non'.

If you do manage to make it into the pool in your normal non-Speedo swimming attire — beware. Sirens will go off, lights will flash, crack squads of lifeguards will hunt you down and haul you out. Well, maybe not lights and sirens but it will almost certainly result in the swimming attendant blowing a whistle, shouting at you and then, if you ignore it, trying to fish you out with a hook.

If all the men in the pool looked like Daniel Craig in his spray-on trunks, women onlookers wouldn't mind, but, by and large, this isn't the case. I love France, I love the people, but some rules are quite strange to me and that is definitely one of them.

7. I'm not telling porkies
You will never find a pig named Napoleon in France; it is against the law.

8. Paul the other one
If you live next door to a Frenchman called Paul, and another neighbour tells you that the villagers have a pet name for him that sounds like Popaul, never ever say it aloud. It means 'dick'. Yes. I did. My neighbour Paul now does not speak to me.

9. No name calling
If you give birth in France you won't be allowed to call your child Fraise (the French word for strawberry) or anything deemed weird that is considered 'contrary to the child's interest' and may encourage excessive teasing. When officially registering a baby's name, the registrar has the power to question the parents' choice if he or she is not happy with it. I kid you not. They're not allowed to just say, 'Oh you can't call her Marie, I've always hated that name', but if they think a name might 'disadvantage' a child in later life

or in the school playground, they can bring it to the attention of the courts and it has to be ruled on. In fact, up until 1993 parents in France had to choose a name for their baby from a long list of acceptable 'prenoms' laid out by authorities.

In 2014 French courts backed a registrar who rejected the name Nutella as a suitable name for a girl. In 2010 a couple of fanatical Michael Jackson fans wanted to call their son MJ, but this too was rejected by the courts who didn't find it a Thriller of a moniker.

The Nutella case was a great source of amusement for the villagers where I live, and there was lots of laughter in the bar as people tried to think of good names to call babies to annoy registrars and officials — some of which are actually real names of celebrity children in the UK and US. It was agreed by unanimous vote that Monsieur Foyard would from now on be known as Monsieur Coin Coin, which means 'quack quack', since he waddles home from the bar after a glass or two of pastis.

10. Beat the system
If you want to do something at a council office, for instance pay a tax bill, or request information about planning permits, make an 11.30 a.m. appointment or get there at

11 a.m. and queue. Nothing makes a bureaucrat miss his or her lunch. Noon is sacred — one *must* have a two-hour lunch break. Nobody knows what happens if they don't take a full two hours — they've never tried it.

11. The customer isn't always right
Don't expect shops to be open from midday until 2 p.m. when you are on your lunch break. The shop is not open for your convenience.

12. Get a word in edgeways
There is no such thing as talking too much in France. French people revere the written and spoken word and will never use one when five hundred will do. I recently went to a jazz concert in Le Touquet with an audience of several hundred. The person at the tourist office whose idea it was to book the act made a ten-minute speech about what jazz is before the musicians came on stage. The largely French audience listened politely and applauded with enthusiasm while the British contingent went to sleep.

13. It's life, Jim, but not as we know it
Never ever tell your French neighbours that you moved to France because it is cheaper

than living in your home country. It will be considered deeply insulting. The fact is there is most likely always somewhere else you can buy an even cheaper property, so it's unlikely to be just about money. If you tell a French person you moved there because you love the way of life, they will be much more accepting of you. I made the mistake of telling my neighbour that I could never have afforded the house and land I have in France if I was still in the UK; he has never forgiven me. These days I talk about how I appreciate the French love of tradition and culture, their patriotism and love of good food and wine, how I can go to a different market every day of the week and buy seasonal goods — and that's the truth of it.

This is what happens when you do it wrong. The person you told will narrow their eyes and nod slowly but say nothing. They will rush to tell everyone else in the village the news that a *salop* (arsehole) has moved into town.

14. Speedy Gonzalez

If you move to the countryside and need internet as a priority, you might want to check the internet service before you buy. In my village we have no mobile phone signal, and the internet goes on and off like a faulty light bulb and when it does work is so slow that it sometimes takes an hour to download a five-minute video. When I spoke to our internet provider and asked for advice they helpfully suggested I move to a town with a fast internet service.

15. Pay the postie
French postmen and women will offer to sell you a rather unattractive post office calendar at Christmas. It's up to you how much you offer. When I asked my postwoman she said, 'As you wish.' Take my advice and give at least 5 euros or your post might be delayed. If, like me, you offer a 20 euro note and expect change, don't. Your friendly postie will hot foot it down the path but you will get a great service for the rest of the year.

16. I get by with a little help from my friends
It's fine to be friends with expats AND French people at the same time! Some expats think it's bad form to have expat friends — it's not; a friend is a friend is a friend.

17. Don't name drop
Don't expect to be on first-name terms for a while. When you're introduced it will often be as Monsieur or Madame this or that and

you're expected to call them that until they tell you to call them by their first name.

18. Chez nous

Don't expect to be offered a look round a French person's house when you visit. It's a particularly British thing that we offer visitors the chance to check out where we live, but in France this is definitely not de rigueur.

P. S. Don't use the term 'de rigueur' in conversation with French people the way you do with English speakers — it doesn't mean quite the same thing. Rather than being trendy it means mandatory.

19. Lend a helping hand

In the countryside be prepared to be a part of the community and live by their rules. We have helped dig potatoes in return for trays of plums and mended a roof in return for firewood. It is never discussed; we never expect anything, helping each other out is normal.

20. The best things in life are free

Volunteering is a great way to make friends and become a part of the community. Whether it's helping out at an animal refuge or a local school or charity, it will go a long way to helping you fit in.

21. No *Blazing Saddles*, **please**

Don't give your French friends baked beans; they will be forever convinced that you have no taste whatsoever.

22. Bringing the bread home

Don't hand someone a loaf of bread upside down, or put it on the table upside down. It's said to invite hunger into the house.

23. Like a bat out of hell

Singing at Halloween will create stormy weather, apparently. According to some French people anyway. If you must sing, do it quietly and not in full view of suspicious locals.

24. Mack the Knife

You must never give a French friend a knife as a gift. They first have to give you a coin so that they 'buy' it from you, therefore saving your friendship from being 'cut'.

25. Water way to carry on

In France it is considered bad luck to cross a stream carrying a cat. If this is something you really feel a need to do, try to do it out of sight of your neighbours, at least.

26. Don't make a fosse about it

It's not uncommon in the French countryside

to have a septic tank — many homes are not connected to mains sewage. There are legal requirements about emptying the tank, such as who does it (they must be authorized) and since 2009 they must provide you with a certificate that the job has been done. When buying a house, ask the seller for proof that the septic tank has been emptied and push the estate agent to get more information about when the tank was installed and that it complies with regulations. In my experience, some estate agents and *notaires* (the equivalent of conveyancing lawyers) gloss over what is a bit of a grey area. Try to get them to confirm in writing that whatever property you're buying complies with current requirements — installing a new septic tank will set you back at least 8,000 euros and will mean a lot of upheaval.

27. Some like it hot

Always think about putting in heating at the beginning of the project when you're renovating a French house. It may seem really romantic when you buy a house with log fires, but this soon wears off when you have to keep cutting and carrying in wood. When it's snowing or very cold you will soon discover you get through your wood pile at a rate of knots. It's quite a physical requirement to chop, store and load and then keep replenishing supplies indoors — especially if you're a bit older. Also, if you're out for the day in winter, you will return to a cold house. If you still want a wood fire, consider additional heating for those really cold times when you need a booster.

28. It's all an act
The day you buy a house you need to sign paperwork called the *acte authentique* — but you can get someone to stand as your proxy if you're not able to do it. I'd recommend you try to make sure you can do it yourself and go to check the house beforehand on the day of the signing. I've heard stories that sellers have removed doors, light switches and all sorts, but once you've signed the document, it's too late to do anything about it. You can stipulate beforehand if you want anything specifically covered. Our house had a rusty old caravan in the back garden and several old freezers were left behind that we had to get rid of, but we could have had a clause to ensure that the vendor disposed of them.

29. You know how to whistle, don't you?
Don't be afraid to visit the town hall and ask for advice — it's what they're there for and I've never ever heard that people went to a

town hall and didn't get advice. In fact, the French hate to say they don't know something. I've had help explaining bills, finding an architect, getting planning permission and sorting out a tax bill I paid but couldn't get the tax office to admit to. The town hall staff made phone calls, copies of bills and explained how we should handle things.

P. S. Always take at least one copy of everything you send or receive. It's almost certain that you'll need to show it several times before you get to the end of your quest if it involves French administration.

30. Learn the rules of boules

Or pétanque as it is also called. France's most popular ball game involves throwing a heavy ball (usually made of steel and marked so you can tell your balls from other players') at a small red *cochonnet*, which translates as piglet but in this case means a small red ball. It is claimed that up to 17 million French people partake of this sport. It's a simple but clever game.

The object is easy: individually, or in two teams of two (doublette) or three (triplette), you toss your balls as close to the *cochonnet* as possible. But, unlike in most games you're allowed, in fact you're encouraged, to interfere with your opponent's balls, knocking them further away from the goal, if you can, with each of your throws. There's no such thing as letting someone win for friendship's sake in France; you need to go all out to win — both the game and the admiration of your new French friends.

We do hope that you have enjoyed reading this large print book.

Did you know that all of our titles are available for purchase?

We publish a wide range of high quality large print books including:
Romances, Mysteries, Classics
General Fiction
Non Fiction and Westerns

Special interest titles available in large print are:
The Little Oxford Dictionary
Music Book
Song Book
Hymn Book
Service Book

Also available from us courtesy of Oxford University Press:
Young Readers' Dictionary
(large print edition)
Young Readers' Thesaurus
(large print edition)

For further information or a free brochure, please contact us at:
Ulverscroft Large Print Books Ltd.,
The Green, Bradgate Road, Anstey,
Leicester, LE7 7FU, England.
Tel: (00 44) 0116 236 4325
Fax: (00 44) 0116 234 0205

Other titles published by Ulverscroft:

FIRE WOMAN

Josephine Reynolds

When seventeen-year-old Josephine Reynolds signed up to the Norfolk Fire Service in 1982, there was no such thing as a firefighter — only firemen. Nevertheless, she was determined to stick it out. From the gruelling fifteen months of training — wrestling 25-metre thrashing, water-spurting hoses, and manoeuvring through pitch-dark, smoke-filled rooms — to her years on the job as a fully-fledged firefighter — tackling forest fires, escaped zoo animals and unexploded bombs — she tells the story of the exhaustion and exhilaration, the grief and camaraderie, of her career with Britain's Fire Service.

DAUGHTER MOTHER ME

Alana Kirk

In life, women can have many labels: daughter, wife, career woman, mother. Alana Kirk has worn them all; and, whilst her life is hectic, she feels in control. Then, four days after the birth of her third daughter, her mother suffers a massive stroke. And just like that, everything changes ... Alana has entered what she terms her 'Sandwich Years' — sandwiched between seeing to the needs of her parents and children: both grieving for, and caring for, her beloved mum; supporting her father; raising her three young daughters; and getting her career back on track. But how long can she continue before the cracks begin to show?

LEAP IN

Alexandra Heminsley

Alexandra Heminsley thought she could swim. She really did. It may have been because she could run, or because she only ever did ten minutes of breaststroke at a time. But, as she learned one day while flailing about in the sea, she really couldn't . . . Believing that the life lived most fully is the one with the most experience packed in, she decides to conquer her fear of the ocean tides. From the ignominy of getting into a wetsuit to the triumph of swimming from Kefalonia to Ithaca, Alex learns that the water is never as frightening once you're in . . .

MAD GIRL

Bryony Gordon

Bryony Gordon is a bestselling author, successful columnist, and happily married mother. She also has OCD. It's the snake in her brain that has told her, ever since she was a teenager, that her world is about to come crashing down: that her family might die if she doesn't repeat a phrase five times, or that she might have murdered someone and forgotten about it. It's caused alopecia, bulimia, and drug dependency. And Bryony is sick of it. Keeping silent about her condition has given it a cachet it simply does not deserve: it's time for her to speak out . . .